GROUNDING SECURITY

Grounding Security

Family, Insurance and the State

CAROL WEISBROD

School of Law, University of Connecticut, USA

Routledge
Taylor & Francis Group
LONDON AND NEW YORK

First published 2006 by Ashgate Publishing

Reissued 2018 by Routledge
2 Park Square, Milton Park, Abingdon, Oxon OX14 4RN
711 Third Avenue, New York, NY 10017, USA

Routledge is an imprint of the Taylor & Francis Group, an informa business

A Library of Congress record exists under LC control number: 2006013335

ISBN 13: 978-0-815-38934-7 (hbk)
ISBN 13: 978-1-351-15704-9 (ebk)

Contents

Preface and Acknowledgments

This book brings together subjects which are, as a group of three, not ordinarily discussed together, though in units of two they may be. Thus family and government are frequently joined: Do governmental policies shape families or are they part of the natural order? Does the health of families have an effect on government? Insurance and government is a subject. (How does government regulate insurance? In what sense can we say that government itself is an insurer?) But in the American law school curriculum the three subjects are conceived quite separately. Insurance is a part of a business curriculum. Family law is traditionally in its own place, off at the side, more recently linked to women and the law and constitutional law. And "government" is divided, depending on the level of government, into courses with titles such as 'Constitutional Law' and 'Local Government Law'. From the point of view of the individual, however, it seems that the three are linked, at least in our expectations, as major sources of individual security. These three are the things on which, in modern America at least, we largely depend when we think about issues of our own safety and security, emotional and financial and the security of those close to us. It is this perspective of the individual, at least as I understand that perspective, which has shaped this book.

I am fortunate in teaching at an institution that is hospitable to inter-disciplinary work, and have a great debt to the Law School of the University of Connecticut and to Dean Nell Newton for intellectual and financial support. As always, the staff of the law school library has provided invaluable assistance. This project has grown out of my association with The Law School's Insurance Law Center, directed by Professor Tom Baker. The Center has provided both assistance and encouragement at various points over several years. The Insurance and Society Discussion Group, one of the activities of the Insurance Law Center, sustains a very broad understanding of the role of insurance and the range of subjects with which it could be associated. Conversations with that group have left their mark on this work.

Additionally, many individuals have contributed one way or another. I would like particularly to thank: Tom Baker, Sean Griffith, Mark Janis, Caroline Jones, Richard Kay, Austin Sarat, Peter Siegelman, Aviam Soifer, and Steven Wilf.

This book, as the work of a generalist, will, I assume, satisfy no specialist. The presentation is less linear than some would like, having too much of the character of pastiche or collage. But juxtaposition is the whole point here, so that we can see the interplay of the ideas of institutions, whether they are classed as public or private, and can get a sense of how the realities of those institutions might sometimes disappoint us. Materials are used not because they are representative or statistically significant but because they are interesting. Resisting the tendency of the legal mind to separate things that are in fact linked (as a line attributed to Thomas Reed Powell has it) the book tries connecting or reconnecting things presently considered apart from each other. To that extent, it is intended to perform a useful function.

Introduction

"Security," we are told, is the word of our age.[1] In the United States, in the current discussion, it may refer to national security and problems of terrorism. Or it may refer to individual security, particularly economic. While other programs are sometimes involved, the discussion at this writing focuses on debates over social security and the program of some in national politics to dismantle the security projects associated with the New Deal. It is this second context that this book addresses, examining three mechanisms traditionally conceived as affording security. The book assumes that the idea of security includes emotional and financial components. These connect and inter-penetrate so that such a common concept as "care taking," can include ideas of emotional and financial support.

It was conventional once to say, in the literature on social security, that there were three legs of the stool that supported income stability in retirement: savings, pensions, and social security.[2] The three are reframed here as family, insurance, and government. At the moment, we tend to describe social security as a government program and to view policies regarding the family in a distinct category, sometimes associated with debates over poverty programs—the security and welfare of the poor—sometimes associated with debates over public morality. The presentation here is a variation of the older approach. It assumes that there are three legs or foundational pillars of individual security: the family, private insurance (one form that the market takes) and government. The essays that follow place these pillars in relation to each other. Further, the discussions consider the ways in which these pillars have changed and are changing. For example, while it is commonly said that at least one of these pillars, the family, is crumbling and not performing its function,[3] the chapter on the family here will urge that the family is being restructured rather than crumbling and that the new structure performs some functions quite well, though others, once associated with the family, are performed much less well.

If it is true of all three of these pillars that they are, if not disintegrating, still changing and changing dramatically, then policy makers—and particularly those associated with the third governmental pillar—should be alert to these changes. If each of the pillars is dependent on the other, then each must, in order to perform

1 *Washington Post* (2005), February 6, p. B1: "Security has become the word of our age: Last week in his State of the Union Speech, President Bush used it 29 times—7 in reference to national security and 22 in discussing Social Security …" (sidebar).

2 Larry DeWitt (1996), "Research note #1: Origins of the Three-Legged Stool Metaphor for Social Security", Social Security Online [website] <http://www.ssa.gov/history/stool.html> (accessed September 7, 2004).

3 Robert Goodin (2000), "Crumbling Pillars: Social Security Futures", *The Political Quarterly* 71, 144–50.

its role, have a clear sense of what that other is doing. For example, in the modern United States, policy rests on basic assumptions about two other institutions, family and private insurance, which also provide security. If key government assumptions are wrong in whole or part, government policy will prove to be inadequate. To the extent that individuals misconceive the shape or strength of the institutions on which they are relying—including the state—they are likely to be injured.

A first chapter offers an overview of the idea of security. The chapter provides a review of the work of I.M. Rubinow, a Russian immigrant to the United States who in his various works examined the connections between families, communities and state, at a more abstract level. An early advocate and publicist of the idea of social insurance, Rubinow lived to see the New Deal and to be disappointed in its conception of the solution to the problem of risk and poverty. To further illustrate the connections between the pillars of security, the chapter moves to a consideration of interactions between family, private organizations, and public organizations in seventeenth-century Holland, whose concerns, as Simon Schama notes in *The Embarrassment of Riches* (1982), were not unlike our own. The chapter examines the life of the seventeenth-century Dutch painter Frans Hals and particularly his final paintings. The general point here is that a historical narrative that sees institutions as succeeding each other, so that guild and unions assume the functions of the family and then states assume the functions of guild/unions, may not be as useful as history that assumes the continuing existence of all of these institutions, some at times more prominent than others in the life of an individual.

Chapter 2 considers the modern American family. The question raised is whether contemporary descriptions of the family as a security-providing entity reflect a solid reality or whether they relate more to an older form of family. The suggestion here is that the family as evoked is not our family. Ours, while it may be deeper emotionally than earlier family forms, is not reliable as a source of security except in particular moments and in particular shapes.

Chapter 3 moves to another foundation of security, private insurance, built once, more than now, on ideas of community and mutual aid. But there are limits to the utility of insurance as a provider of security and even the insurance risk analysis may itself not be as useful as it once was.

"Social security" and various forms of public assistance in the United States are treated in Chapter 4. State provision of security—called social security in the United States—is primarily linked to employment. Because of this, many people are not included in the social security system. The history of other kinds of security provision, such as welfare, reveal that American commitment to the idea of government as the provider of security is much less intense than it is in some European countries.

Chapter 5 attempts to argue for public responsibility for security on liberal assumptions. If the self is as plural as any society, (as was urged in earlier work),[4] the need is to structure the state umbrella so that entrances, exits and reentries are

---

4 See Carol Weisbrod (2002), *Emblems of Pluralism* (Princeton, NJ: Princeton University Press).

considered not as exceptions or failures of commitment, but rather as aspects of the complex human situation.

The "primal scene" on issues of security is the expulsion from Eden.[5] We have many images of life Before the Fall, before the temptation and its consequences: death, scarcity, and conflict and the world which in its totality we call The Human Condition. Our entire situation is After the Fall and our search for security exists against the background of an idea of something different and better. This is an old observation, made, for example, by the historian of the social security administration in his paper on social security. "You might say," he noted that "the search for security began when Adam and Eve were driven from the shelter of the Garden of Eden."[6] And of course we might link our search to theories of the search for perfect integration represented by the womb. It might follow from this search for integration and security that attempts to provide security would be focused on somehow getting back into the Garden, to the relation of perfect trust and harmony that we are told was the essential character of Eden.

But, in general, this is not what political Utopias are doing. Rather, Utopian thinking tends to be looking at a world after the fall. As H.G. Wells put, it in *A Modern Utopia*, he was not talking about a re-made world or a re-made man in the manner of William Morris. Rather, he was assuming the ordinary man; in effect, in a world of realistic risks. "We are to restrict ourselves first to the limitations of human possibility as we know them in the men and women of this world today, and then to all the inhumanity, all the insubordination of nature. We are to shape our state in a world of uncertain seasons, sudden catastrophes, antagonistic diseases, and inimical beasts and vermin, out of men and women with like passions, like uncertainties of mood and desire to our own." Moreover, Wells insisted, "we are going to accept this world of conflict, to adopt no attitude of renunciation towards it, to face it in no ascetic spirit, but in the mood of the Western peoples, whose purpose is to survive and overcome. So much we adopt in common with those who deal not in Utopias, but in the world of Here and Now."[7]

This inquiry operates in the world of Here and Now, considering the past when that is useful for understanding how we got to what we take to be "here."

But concern here is not only focused on advice to policy makers. Precisely because the third governmental pillar changes also, one is forced to consider these issues not merely in terms of policies that governments might adopt (and then abandon) but in terms of the choices individuals face when dealing with the uncertainties involved in all three pillars. To the degree that the discussion attempts to address the three

5 Genesis, Chapters 2 and 3, Herbert May and Bruce Metzger (eds) (1962), *Oxford Annotated Bible* (revised standard). (New York: Oxford University Press).

6 Abe Bortz (n.d.), "Special Study #1: Abe Bortz Lecture on the History of Social Security: Historical Development of the Social Security Act", Social Security Online [website] http://ssa.gov/history/bortz.html (accessed July 9, 2004).

7 H.G. Wells (1967[1905]), A *Modern Utopia* (Lincoln, NE: University of Nebraska Press), pp. 7-8.

pillars from outside all of them, from the point of view of an individual's attempting to ground security for themselves through these pillars, it is a kind of self-help book. The effort is not to outline the failings of individuals who have made bad choices, or to analyze the misconceptions that led them to those choices with an emphasis on ways they might have done better. This need not be a discussion that translates into something about blaming the victim. Rather, the point is to say that in the end there are only individual choices, made against the backgrounds of institutions such as family, corporations and states. To the extent that we want informed choices—and are willing to subject ourselves to the risk of information overload and the anxiety of recurrent uncertainties—we will want to consider the risks associated with each of the pillars as we make choices directed to the future.

Chapter 1

Pillars of Security

1. Economic hazards give rise to a great deal of worry which often assumes the acute form of fear.

2. The apprehension of the ever-present economic hazards does result in a great deal of foresight—in the striving to achieve some degree of security against the threatening doom through personal efforts.

3. But for the vast majority of people, all these measures of individual foresight prove entirely futile, so that out of this realization of the futility of personal foresight there arises a quest for security, to be achieved in some social, collective way.

I.M. Rubinow[1]

This book deals with security and insecurity, rather than wealth and poverty. That is, it deals with the mechanisms that people use to keep themselves from poverty or the apprehension of poverty, and also of accidents, illness and injuries, which may jeopardize their economic positions.

The "people" may be anyone, rich or poor. The rich are anxious because they may lose their wealth and become less wealthy, the poor are anxious because they will become impoverished, or may be caught in a situation so hopeless that they are not anxious at all. Both "rich" and "poor" could involve us in definitional issues, though in America we are particularly concerned with the definitions of poverty because our public assistance programs have tended to require "need" and sometimes "worthiness" in addition to need.[2] (American social security payments are given to those who show not need but a specific history of covered employment, which can be seen as a surrogate for worthiness.) As the late Charles Black pointed out, we spend a good deal of time on "where do we draw the line" issues here, more people worrying about this question than about the question of how to feed hungry children.[3]

It is easy to concede the relative aspects of poverty. DeTocqueville said some time ago: "the English poor may appear almost rich to the French poor and the

---

1 I.M. Rubinow (1934), *The Quest for Security* (New York: Henry Holt), p. 31.

2 For a discussion of the exceptionalism of the US system, see Jill Quadagno (1987), "Theories of the Welfare State", *Annual Review of Sociology*, 13, 109–28.

3 Charles Black (1997), *A New Birth of Freedom* (New York: Putnam), p. 136.

latter are so regarded by the Spanish poor."[4] American poor are well off by some standards. But this point, going to "wants" and "needs", assumes that something called a basic need actually is there to be filled. And this need—these needs—are not filled in the United States today for everyone. Moreover, many more are fearful that given certain circumstances, these needs will not be filled for them. The old who looked for security in continuing care environments, investing for the long term in institutions that sometimes went bankrupt, were left without resources of their own. A day laborer in the line-ups in New York City is quoted as saying that she works to eat.[5]

The issue of insecurity necessarily then involves a discussion of an American approach to the poor and to welfare. But it also involves a discussion of American ideas of success and achievement, particularly when we operate at a high level of abstraction and stress that the "risks" of life are risks to which we are all subject. Some who are in some sense "secure" may feel themselves constantly "at risk" in the sense that they regularly expose themselves to the possibility of failure by undertaking projects that may not be successful. They may not therefore achieve to the level of their ambition. Others who have achieved relative security see themselves driven by risk avoidance rather than ambition. They may seek a quiet life.

As a general matter, it is thought that individuals are not good at risk assessment, over-valuing anecdotal evidence at the expense of statistical evidence, influenced by the massive amount of information, advocacy and advertising emanating from interest groups relating to specific risks and particular solutions.[6] And there is danger everywhere: "How can you tabulate the endless dangers of tobacco, of food preservatives, asbestos, the stuff that crops are sprayed with—*E.coli* from raw chicken on the hands of employees ..."[7]

Among the dangers everywhere are the instabilities in the mechanisms offered as remedies for danger. In this book, the focus is on the particular solutions offered by family, insurance and government that are intended to provide security. It is not that these mechanisms do nothing. It is rather that they too often do not do what they are said to do.

One tendency in the United States is to respond by saying that additional information, creating an informed choice, will produce better decisions on such questions. But here it has been noted that too much information, an information

4 Alexis DeTocqueville (1997), *Memoir on Pauperism* (Chicago: Ivan Dee). See on this work G. Himmelfarb, (1984[1983]), *The Idea of Poverty: England in the Early Industrial Age* (New York: Knopf), p. 147 ff.

5 Nina Bernstein (2005), "Invisible to Most, Women Line up for Day Labor", *New York Times*, 15 August, Section A, col. 4.

6 Mary Douglas and Aaron Wildavsky (1983), *Risk and Culture* (Berkeley, CA: University of California Press); on financial risks particularly, see Robert J. Shiller (1999), "Social security and institutions for intergenerational, intragenerational, and international risk-sharing", *Carnegie-Rochester Conference Series on Public Policy* 50: 165–204, Nicholas Taleb (2005), "Scaring us Senseless", *New York Times*, 24 July, Section 4, p. 13.

7 Saul Bellow (2000), *Ravelstein* (New York: Viking), p. 44.

overload, may produce a world in which there are not enough hours in the day to make "informed choices" as to the many things we are expected to choose. As Jon Elster argued in another context, the factors to be dealt with may be so complex that we are arguably just as well off choosing randomly.[8]

This book is a general discussion of the ways in which people look at particular institutions, stressing particular religious and economic ideologies that frame the issues involved. And it is a picture of the ways in which certain instruments of security do not reliably provide it.[9] The book discusses "the poor" at times because the mechanisms for security are designed to protect people from the worst consequences of risks, among them destitution. It is not a statistical picture of marriage and divorce in America, or of public and private insurance, or of the amounts of money spent by the US Government on public assistance programs. It is not a full picture of the New Deal.

Each chapter of this book uses as a motto a quotation from Isaac Max Rubinow. Rubinow's observations and arguments are threaded through the discussion. Rubinow seems to have been unusual in that he had direct knowledge of the different solutions available to the problem of insecurity. In 1913, Rubinow published *Social Insurance*.[10] He is identified in his various biographies as a social worker and statistician. He also worked with B'nai Brith and various other organizations. For several years, he worked as a doctor in Palestine with Henrietta Szold. He died at 61, in 1936.

Rubinow is highlighted first for his importance as a figure in the early twentieth century history of social security in the United States, and second because of his particular perspective on security. He saw clearly the role (and the limits) of the various institutions that are used by individuals to find their own security. Rubinow's disappointment in the federal social security program—announced on the day that *The Quest for Security* was published—was profound.[11] His sense that the family could not be relied on was obvious and his understanding of the limits of private charity—his own experience was in the world of Jewish communal organizations—was deep.

Rubinow's lifelong concern with the subject of security is evident. It is not clear, however, how he got to it. He was not from the Jewish masses, who arrived impoverished in the New World and sometimes remained so for a generation or more. He was not from the trade union movement. His family was somehow wealthy enough to send him to school and in fact professional school. He was financially comfortable enough to change professional direction, from medicine to statistics. He arrived in February 1893, entered the junior year of Columbia University, and graduated in 1895. His interests were then in biology and he took a 1-year

---

8 Jon Elster (1989), *Solomonic Judgments* (Cambridge: Cambridge University Press).

9 Materials are easily available detailing the support that is provided and the current controversies.

10 I.M. Rubinow (1913), *Social Insurance* (New York: Henry Holt).

11 See Chapter 4 below.

postgraduate study in biology as university scholar in Columbia (1895–96). "I took up the study of medicine at the same time at New York University Medical College, receiving my M.D. in 1898. Practiced medicine from 1899 to 1903, when I have definitely given it up in order to go in for statistics and social science."[12] None of this resonates with an impoverished background.

Rubinow does not, however, seem to have been caught up in the guilt that, Professor Thomas Haskell suggests, motivated some of the American progressives, who understood that their comfort depended on someone else's deprivation.[13] Nor does one see in Rubinow the direct and sometimes fanatic hatred of money and commercial society that one sometimes finds in the writing of reformers and moralists.[14] In general, Rubinow's target was not money or commerce but a structure that failed to recognize the dignity of individuals. The theme of dignity is found also in current writing concerned with issues of poverty and security. Thus, in the current book of Ackerman and Alsott on stakeholding we see references to shame, embarrassment, and humiliation.[15]

It is the question of dignity and reciprocal looking ("the gaze", after all, can work in two directions) that I would like to illustrate here with a discussion of the seventeenth-century Dutch painter Frans Hals. Initially, however, some general discussion of security may be useful.

Security Overview

Objective measures of poverty, or objective quantified values for conditions producing (objective) security or insecurity are not the subject. Here, it is entirely likely that poor Americans live more comfortably than the poor of the depression, or that poor Americans of the twenty-first century live in greater comfort than the rich of previous centuries, who might well have lived in luxury but not comfort.[16] Rather, it considers the observations of various writers who have thought about the need for a sense of security as a condition of human existence. Security is treated as a psychological necessity in the same way that food or air are physical necessities.

---

12 Original autobiographical statement is in the Isaac M. Rubinow collection, Cornell University Library #5616, Box 8, Folder 40, 4 pp. Rubinow described himself as a socialist in 1916, referring to a 20-year membership in the American Socialist Party. Roy Lubove (1968), *The Struggle for Social Security* (Cambridge, MA: Harvard University Press, p. 194, n. 37) writes that "the Russian Revolution would upset Rubinow's socialist convictions."

13 Thomas Haskell (2001), *Emergence of Professional Social Science: The Emergence of Professional Social Science and the Nineteenth Century and the Crisis of Authority* (Baltimore, MD: Johns Hopkins Press).

14 See for example, Herman Melville (2004), *Typee* (Boston, MA: Houghton Mifflin), pp. 127–8.

15 Bruce Ackerman and Anne Alstott (1999), *The Stakeholder Society* (New Haven, CT: Yale University Press).

16 See the Alexis de Tocqueville discussion in *Memoir on Pauperism* (ed. Gertrude Himmelfarb).

(The physical and the psychological may be linked in a way that suggests that they may both be physical.) "Life is a difficult and serious business," Ernest Gellner says. "The protection from starvation and insecurity is not easily achieved ..."[17] Gellner's comment—he moves on to refer to the importance of government in achieving security—makes the first central point. While we take as a starting point that life is good, that one should choose life, we are also told that "life is not a bowl of cherries," "It's a great life if you don't weaken" and that, as the old joke has it, while it might be better not to have been born, who of us can be so lucky? In short, we are repeatedly told that even in the best of circumstances, getting through our allotted time is not easy. It is only a failure of imagination that permits individuals and perhaps not so many at that to tell themselves that bad things happen only to other people.[18]

Security is understood sometimes to have a privileged position among our values. John Stuart Mill made the point this way: "Security, [is] to every one's feelings the most vital of all interests." Mill continued by contrasting security to various other worldly goods: "Nearly all other earthly benefits are needed by one person, not needed by another; and many of them can, if necessary, be cheerfully foregone, or replaced by something else." But, there was one of which this was not true: "Security no human being can possibly do without." We depend on security "for the whole value of all and every good, beyond the passing moment." This is because "nothing but the gratification of the instant could be of any worth to us, if we could be deprived of everything the next instant by whoever was momentarily stronger than ourselves."[19]

The images we have from Hobbes, that life is nasty, brutish, and short,[20] give rise also to the image of the competitive loner, the one who is committed to self-preservation at all cost, perhaps not even with an exception in favor of a child. The anthropologist Colin Turnbull's Ik—a tribe of starving individuals who would not even protect their own infants—present the image of totally self-interested loners.[21] The images are powerful, whether or not accurate. They are reinforced by related images of human beings in extreme situations, in which the fight for survival is the re-enactment among the civilized of the most primitive struggles of the race.

The image of the loner is not, however, the only one we have. We often insist that human beings live in society, and we have then the idea that human beings are necessarily and intrinsically social, living with other people, involved in projects of mutual support and aid. Three particular mechanisms of cooperation for security, family insurance and government, are linked. We know this not only because

17 Ernest Gellner (1964), "Nationalism", in Ernest Gellner, *Thought and Change*, pp. 147–53 (Chicago: University of Chicago Press).

18 Or to people who deserve to have bad things happen to them. See the discussion in Chapter 4 below.

19 John Stuart Mill (1991[1859]), "Utilitarianism", in *On Liberty and Other Essays*. (Oxford: Oxford University Press), pp. 131–90.

20 Thomas Hobbes (1962), *The Leviathan* (New York: Collier Books, Macmillan Publishing).

21 Colin Turnbull (1972), *The Mountain People* (New York: Simon and Schuster).

formal and official public policies makes reference to these links—as when William Beveridge refers to the three pillars of social security[22]—but because the popular images of instruments of security make reference to these links. Thus, when Robert Heinlein, the libertarian science fiction writer, insists that there is no social security in his libertarian world, he assumes the existence of a larger intergenerational family which will look after the elderly:[23] When Leon Blum wrote his proposal for marriage—no marriage before 30, after a period of sexual experimentation for men and women—he assumed (long term) a state that would look after any children and also a large strong family.[24]

It is possible to approach the sequence of institutions in a way in which "the composition of the group cushioning the impact of individual catastrophes shifted over time from kinship networks to church and guild, to ethnic and trade based mutuals and to the immediate precursors of the insurance giants that protect us today."[25] But it is also possible to see these structures as coexisting, then and to a lesser degree now, with the insurance institutions. While the old guilds have become unions that themselves use insurance companies to provide coverage for members, family and church clearly are in the background when, for example, insurance fails to protect.

Some ideas of security are so linked to class as to be largely descriptive of the life of a class: "I knew Lord Salisbury well, and was very fond of him," an upper-class English woman wrote. She continues:

> I married his fourth son in 1894, an age that seems as far away to us now as the Norman Conquest. And if I am going to talk about Lord Salisbury, I must say something about the time, not only the 1894 time, but really the whole period until the First World War, because that was a complete section of history. And the first thing I think I ought to say is that you have no idea how comfortable we were.

She elaborates her precise meaning:

> I do not mean to say in our circumstances, that is according to whether we were well off or not, but how comfortable we were in our minds and how safe. You might fall off a horse, you might have a railway accident, you might be drowned out swimming; but those were personal accidents, painful no doubt, but nothing fell on you from the sky. You had no insecurity—you were perfectly safe.[26]

---

22 William Beveridge (1943), *The Pillars of Security* (New York: Macmillan).

23 See Robert Heinlein (1966), *The Moon is a Harsh Mistress* (New York: Orb).

24 Leon Blum (1907), *Du Mariage* (Paris: Albin Michel). (Of course there would be few such children, he thought, because of the availability of contraception.)

25 Tom Baker (1994), "Constructing the Insurance Relationship: Sales Stories and Insurance Contract Damages", *Texas Law Review* 72, 1395–738, p. 1414 (acknowledging Ken Casebeer).

26 Viscountess Milner (1956), "Remembering Lord Salisbury", *The Listener*, May 24, p. 679. Thanks to Hugh Macgill for this reference.

Many date the end of that class-oriented security in England with the First World War, but presumably this is not to be assumed for all places. Thus, Mencken described the "interior security" of the aristocrat. The chief "visible evidence of that security is the freedom that goes with it—not only freedom to act, the divine right of the aristocrat to do what he damn well pleases so long as he does not violate the primary guarantees and obligations of his class, but also and more importantly freedom in thought, the liberty to try and error, the right to be his own man."[27] The defect he saw in the United States was the lack of a civilized aristocracy.[28]

The psychological dimensions of security are clear. Martha Minow, reviewing Mary Ann Glendon's 1981 work on *The New Family and the New Property*, noted that an overemphasis on material definitions of security tended to divert our attention from both the issue of the quality of care, for example, and of the importance of other, emotional forms of security.[29] And sometimes, the idea is that too much security is not a good thing. "Apart from war, modern civilization has aimed increasingly at security," Bertrand Russell noted, and then added, "but I am not at all sure that the elimination of all danger makes for happiness."[30] On the whole, however, our efforts are towards security, sometimes defined by the contrast to insecurity.

The idea of insecurity is common in the work of psychologists (for example, Erich Fromm's *Escape from Freedom*). The radical psychologist R.D. Laing used ideas of security and insecurity to treat existential conditions. "A man may have a sense of his presence in the world as a real, alive, whole, and, in a temporal sense, continuous person. As such, he can live out into the world and meet others: a world and others experienced as equally real, alive, whole, and continuous." That person was not, however, the focus of Laing's work. He was interested in "the issues involved where there is partial or almost complete absence of the assurances derived from an existential position of what I shall call primary ontological security." His work described "Primary ontological insecurity," and "the consequent attempts to deal with such anxieties and dangers."[31]

José Ortega argued for the utility of real insecurity:

> To-day, by the very fact that everything seems possible to us, we have a feeling that the worst of all is possible: retrogression, barbarism, decadence. This of itself would not be a

---

27 H.L. Mencken (1982[1949]), *A Mencken Chrestomathy: His Own Selection of His Choicest Writings* (Vintage, New York), Section X, pp. 169–83, 'American Culture', p. 180.

28 Ibid., p. 178.

29 Martha Minow (1982), "The Properties of Family and the Families of Property", *Yale Law Journal* 92, 376–95 (reviewing Glendon (1981), *The New Family and the New Property*. (Toronto: Butterworth)).

30 Bertrand Russell (1960[1949]), *Authority and the Individual* (Boston, MA: Boston Press). "The problem of making peace with our anarchic impulses is one which has been too little studied, but one which becomes more and more imperative as scientific technique advances" (p. 9).

31 R.D. Laing, (1999[1960]), *The Divided Self: An Existential Study in Sanity and Madness* (New York: Routledge), p. 40.

> bad symptom; it would mean that we are once again forming contact with that insecurity which is essential to all forms of life, that anxiety both dolorous and delicious contained in every moment, if we know how to live it to its innermost core, right down to its palpitating vitals.[32]

Generally he said:

> we strain in the attempt to find security and to render ourselves insensible to the fundamental drams of our destiny, by steeping it in habits, usages, topics—in every kind of chloroform. It is an excellent thing, then, that for the first time for nearly three centuries we are surprised to find ourselves with the feeling that we do not know what is going to happen to-morrow.

And he commented in a later work:

> We may regard security as one of man's effort-saving devices. Precaution, anxiety, dread, which rise from insecurity, are forms of effort, an answer, as it were, to nature's imposition upon man.[33]

Insecurity is an idea well known in the popular culture. We analyze the behaviour of a show-off by saying that he is compensating for his insecurities.

Thus the idea "security" has both psychological and material dimensions and one question is whether these can be separated. In theory, at least, it is possible. As we have the paranoid who has enemies, we have the psychologically insecure person who "has," as we say, everything. And we have the secure person who "has" nothing. The mendicant priest, wandering through religious narratives in so many cultures, whose trust is in providence or others along the way represents this pattern.

But in ordinary life, the ideas are often quite intertwined. When we speak of "peace and security" we mean both freedom from the objective realities of war, the threat of violence and physical need and also an inner ease. Objective and subjective security we might say.

The psychological meanings of poverty cannot be dealt with easily. Our own version of it, focusing on the combined issues of poverty and racism, poverty and exclusion,[34] poverty and rejection, is not the only version.

We could talk about the hopelessness of the people whose poverty is "absolute," a "condition of life so characterized by malnutrition, illiteracy, disease, squalid

---

32 Jose Ortega Y. Gasset (1932), *The Revolt of the Masses*. (New York: London: W.W. Norton), p. 45.

33 Jose Ortega Y. Gasset (1961[1941]), *History as a System and other Essays Toward a Philosophy of History* (New York, London: W.W. Norton), p. 106.

34 See particularly Pierre Rosanvallon (2000), *The New Social Question* (trans. Barbara Harshav) (Princeton, NJ: Princeton University Press).

surroundings, high infant mortality and low life expectancy as to be beneath any reasonable definition of human decency."[35]

But no one starves in America. We have said that for some time, and continue to say it. Often we associate poverty and insecurity with the exclusion imposed on racial minorities.[36] But we also know that there is poverty in the dominant racial group, sometimes understood as a regional phenomenon. What then would the psychological issues be, or have been, if we did not stress racism and the consequences of slavery or the isolation of Appalachia? In a society built on upward mobility, what do we say about poverty as a point of origin in general? Is it only that the rich have more, even much more, money?

Here, we have, for example, the account offered by James Reade. Like others, Reade notes that the rich, "not only have money, they have freedom."[37] And he is specific about the relation to the wage earner. The man of property has great bargaining strength, since he "can snap his fingers at those on whom he relies for income. For he can always rely for a time on his capital."[38] Reade stresses the sense of possibility that those who are "secure" feel. This confidence, even when unaccompanied by wealth, is strikingly lacking in those who have neither money nor access to those with money. There is no point in going to parents, or to banks. For the rich, by contrast, there may be the comfortable assumption that every person, and certainly every doorman, will provide assistance if asked. The idea that a human being may simply have nothing with which to negotiate, nothing to offer, no one to call, lacking both power and influence, may be utterly beyond the imagination of those who have never missed a meal.[39]

Then there are the pathologies of poverty, suggested for example in a discussion in Sennett and Dobb, in *The Hidden Injuries of Class*. A man born in poverty who has made it into the middle class is still obsessed by the disorder and even violence of his childhood, when he was surrounded by adults who had no self restraint. Sennett and Cobb write of a man who understood poverty not in terms of deprivation but in terms of lack of self-control. The people who had nothing materially acted like animals. "A poor man therefore has to want upward mobility to achieve dignity in his own life." Dignity is understood to mean acting in an emotionally restrained way.[40]

Certainly money can't buy happiness. Certainly the poor can be happy. Rubinow had done a brief overview of the issue in his 1934 book. It is difficult to be happy if chronically anxious about money. We have Margaret Mead's 1943 discussion of

---

35 Peter Singer (2004), *One World: The Ethics of Globalization*, 2nd edn. (New Haven, CT: Yale University Press), p. 81, quoting Robert McNamera in World Bank (1978), *World Bank, World Development Report, 1978*. (New York: World Bank), p. 111.

36 See Martin Gilens (1999), *Why Americans Hate Welfare* (Chicago: University of Chicago).

37 Quoted in Ackerman and Alstott, *The Stakeholder Society*, p.25.

38 Quoted in Ibid., p. 25.

39 For a discussion of the limits of empathy, see Ian Shapiro (2002), "Why Don't the Poor Soak the Rich?", *Daedelus* 131:1.

40 Richard Sennett and Jonathan Cobb (1972), *The Hidden Injuries of Class* (New York: Vintage), p. 22.

the psychology of those at the time of the depression, both those who were on relief and those who were not, stressing the change in the world in which it was no longer possible to say that virtue was rewarded, that wealth proved one's goodness. All of this was only possible when work was always possible[41] and upward mobility, as represented by the rags to riches fiction of Horatio Alger or the real-life story of John Jacob Astor, is taken as a real option, always. In status societies, Mead says, the emphasis is on who one is. In a free modern society, the emphasis is on what one does. The underlying assumption is, of course, that it is always possible to do something (see Chapter 4 for further discussion of this idea). There is always work, opportunity, the West, the army, something that can be done. Chronic poverty, on such a view, involves a failure to solve a problem where solutions are at hand if one has the wit to see them. Failure is therefore always an individual failure and success is, correspondingly, an individual achievement, based on skill, intelligence, planning and so on. Luck and chance provide opportunity but the deft exploitation of opportunity is an individual virtue.

Other descriptions focus on more lasting aspects of deprivation. James Michener said:

> I am a depression Quaker who has seen the terror that a lack of money can evoke, and for this I make no apology … I have lived my life as if it were all going to fall apart two weeks from now. The urgency stems from some devastating experiences in childhood … So money remains one more life problem which I have not been able to solve with any distinction.[42]

There are complexities in the idea of security that root in an apparent contradiction. The United States is, objectively, one of the more secure countries—even after 9/11—yet we are deeply insecure psychologically. Some of our consumer culture, that culture that creates the objective relative security, is driven by the sale of yet further devices to foster security. Buy this and you will be safe. Perhaps ultimately it is about a desire for immortality. Have this test or procedure and you will live forever, at least to 100.

Frans Hals

The seventeenth-century Dutch painter Frans Hals (b. Antwerp, 1582–83, d. Haarlem, 1666) may be used to illustrate interactions between family, private groups and official groups in a context in which all three sectors of society are operating in a remote though still recognizable world. That world is an early modern commercial society that was the precursor of our own world. Thus, it has been noted that "as

---

41 Margaret Mead (2000[1965]), *And Keep your Powder Dry, An Anthropologist Look at America.* (New York: Berghan Books), p. 76.

42 John P. Hayes (1984), *James Michener: A Biography* (New York: Bobbs-Merrill), p. 9.

everyone knows, modern commercial society first arose in Holland."[43] And Simon Schama, in *The Embarrassment of Riches*, indicates unambiguously that he is writing of a culture whose concerns are very much like his own.[44]

Figure 1.1 Regentesses of The Old Men's Almshouse. Reproduced with permission of the Franz-Hals Museum (Haarlem, Netherlands)

If we have in Holland the precursor to a modern commercial society, we may also have a precursor to the interaction of institutions to protect those who fall between the cracks of that society. We are told, thus, that "the Dutch have been at the cutting edge of welfare policy for the past three hundred years."[45] What we see in the life of Frans Hals is the interaction of precisely the institutions which, in a somewhat different institutional form, we would see today. We can start with the description of E. Gombrich who opens with not the artist but the hierarchy: "There were local committees and governing boards, prominent in the life of Dutch cities, which followed the praiseworthy custom of having their group portraits painted for

43 James Q.Whitman (1994), "The Disease of Roman Law: A Century Later", *Syracuse Journal of International Law and Commerce* 20: 227–34.

44 Simon Schama (1982), *The Embarrassment of Riches: An Interpretation of Dutch Culture in the Golden Age* (Berkeley, CA; University of California Press), p. xi.

45 Charles Parker (1998), *The Reformation of Community: Social Welfare and Calvinist Charity in Holland, 1572–1620*. (Cambridge: Cambridge University Press), p. 8.

the board-rooms and meeting-places of their worshipful companies." An artist who appealed to the public and served this community "hope[d] for a reasonably steady income." "But, the risk was that once his manner ceased to be fashionable, however, he might face ruin."[46]

Gombrich notes that "the first outstanding master of free Holland, Frans Hals, was forced to lead such a precarious existence ..." Hals's parents had left the southern Netherlands because they were Protestants and had settled in the prosperous Dutch city of Haarlem. Gombrich reviews parts of the history: Hals "frequently owed money to his baker or shoemaker. In his old age—he lived to be over eighty—he was granted a small pittance by the municipal almshouse, whose board of governors he painted." As to the board of governors, Gombrich had this to say of the context of group portraits:

> The citizens of the proudly independent towns of the Netherlands had to do their turn in serving as militiamen, usually under the command of the most prosperous inhabitants. It was the custom in the city of Haarlem to honor the officers of these units after their stint of duty with a sumptuous banquet, and it had also become a tradition to commemorate these happy events in a large painting.[47]

Hals, Gombrich tells us, had a special talent here. "It was surely no easy matter for an artist to record the likenesses of so many men within one frame without the result looking stiff or contrived—as earlier efforts invariably did."

Gombrich thinks that "Hals understood from the beginning how to convey the spirit of the jolly occasion." The Dutch painter knew:

> how to bring life into such a ceremonial group without neglecting the purpose of showing each of the twelve members present so convincingly that we feel we must have met them: from the portly colonel who presides at the end of the table, raising his glass, to the young ensign on the opposite side who is not accorded a seat, but proudly looks out of the picture as if he wants us to admire his splendid outfit.

But Gombrich can not quite get away from the economic context in which the work was done. "Perhaps we can admire his mastery even more when we look at one of the magnificent portraits that brought so little money to Hals and his family." But immediately he returns to the painting. "Compared to earlier portraits, it looks almost like a snapshot ... The portraits of Hals give us the impression that the painter has 'caught' his sitter at a characteristic moment and fixed it forever on canvas."[48] He will stress the skill, but the indigence creeps in.

We know here, from this description, that the only oddity in the Hals's story is the point that such a master was so poor. The prominent citizen seems to be so because

---

46 E.H. Gombrich (2002[1995]), *The Story of Art*. London/Newport: Phaidon), p. 414.

47 Ibid., p. 47.

48 Ibid., p. 416.

of his actual worth. The happy occasions are obviously so; the jolly dinners and the rest seem to be so in their nature.[49]

For others, there are more ambiguities in these group portraits. All is perhaps not quite so right with the world, and some art historians have seen complexities in the paintings that are not suggested in the Gombrich account.

The Regents and Regentesses of the Almshouse

Frans Hals was born in a family of modest means and died destitute, someone without family wealth to provide a buffer. His work was not highly valued until long after his death. The family he was born into, as much as the family he created, 10 children with two wives, was a family that needed support as much as providing it. Of course, if he had been born into a wealthy family, much of what happened would have been different, as much as if he had lived in a society that, identifying talented children early because they were needed for the state (the janissaries in Turkey for example), would have removed him from the exigencies of his actual normal life and assisted his work and development.[50] He might have lived in a world that followed Beethoven's recommendation, and permitted artists to deposit their works in an archive while providing the composers with a stipend.[51] But he lived in a commercial society in which artists like others had to earn a living by pleasing a public, perhaps by creating a public. (E.H. Gombrich, while noting that Hals was not always favored, nonetheless is comfortable with the idea that the most famous works are also in many ways and by many standards, the greatest.[52])

Family—his background family and his own family—is critical in understanding his life. Two children were "in care", as we might say, one for incapacity, one for immorality. The support of 10 children was largely beyond him. As it was, Frans Hals married twice, had 10 children, had difficulties with creditors and possibly went through bankruptcy. He had complex relations for decades with the artists' guild, or corporation, which both assisted him and sanctioned him for taking a student from another artist, Judith Leyster. (The early guilds, as has been noted, had among their functions shielding members from risks as well as monitoring the behavior of members at least in certain areas.) After a period of solvency, Hals died in his

---

49 Gombrich knew which faces were intelligent and which were stupid. Ibid., p. 381.

50 Margaret Mead suggests that under the American approach, the issue of where you begin in life affects the judgment of success, so that Americans take into account, and perhaps even discount, significant advantages in life, and forgive a certain failure to reach the summit because of a kind of handicap (Margaret Mead, 2000[1965]). It seems true that careers open to talent is an idea more realized in the United States than elsewhere. But it may be that exactly because of this, failures are not forgiven. See Chapter 5 below.

51 A. Eaglefield-Hull (ed.) (1972), *Beethoven's Letters* (trans. J.S. Shedlock) (New York: Dover), letter of January 15 ["or something like that"] 1801, p. 26.

52 Gombrich, *The Story of Art*, p. 8.

eighties, probably not, however, living in the Haarlem Almshouse that became the Hals museum.

At the end of his life, Hals was commissioned to do two group portraits of the regents and regentesses of the Haarlem Almshouse (*The Regents of the Almshouse* and *Regentesses of The Old Men's Almshouse*). (He had already done the militia group portraits.) While there is considerable speculation—though not in the Gombrich discussion cited above—about his intention in these portraits, whether as Sheila Muller puts it, he was trying to send up the Dutch overseers, we will of course never know.[53] And much of what we think of as casting stones, however obliquely, is in the eyes of a beholder. A later picture by Backer of the regentesses of an Amsterdam orphanage that shows elegantly dressed ladies and ragged children put those governors in a bad light by modern standards, but presumably this is an altogether anachronistic reading.[54]

People seem to agree that Hals was paid well for these two pictures and it is sometimes suggested that the commissions were themselves a kind of charity from the almshouse. At a national portrait gallery, one focuses on the way in which the artist has dealt with the subject; at an art museum one may be more interested in the painter, or in some cases, both the painter and sitter. But here we are concerned with a relationship. Art historians offer various perspectives on this judgment, beginning with the idea that we should not too quickly assume that Hals was negative about his sitters, or that they were critical of him.

Many different questions can be raised about the paintings. We might want to know something about the biography of the painter, or the institutions, the guild, the family, in which he lived and work; or the political context that made possible in Holland, a form—the group portrait—that apparently existed nowhere else. Here, the almshouse is a creature of the municipality and can represent the state. We might be interested in the details of the Dutch welfare system, public and private.

The guilds are said to have been involved in assistance to the poor and we are told, for example, that the redesigned Haarlem St Lukes guild, of which Hals was a member, had a poor box for widows and orphans. The guild, which is often discussed in terms of its monitoring of the work and conditions of work of its members (so that Hals was disciplined, for example, for taking a student from Judith Leyster), also apparently did give some "support." It forgave Hals guild dues for a number of years, for example. And a petition to the guild, by Hals and others, on behalf of an impoverished painter who was not a member, gives an idea of what else the guild might do.[55]

53 Sheila Muller (1985), *Charity in the Dutch Republic: Pictures of Rich and Poor for Charitable Institutions* (Ann Arbor, MI: UMI Research Press). Muller's argument in general is that "Hals is not so engaged in sending up his sitters as he is in revealing what they perceive the Active life to be" (p. 48).

54 Schama, *The Embarrassment of Riches*, p. 575.

55 In general see Max Weber.

It is noted that there is no documentary evidence for the idea that Hals became a resident of the Almshouse.[56] Sheila Muller has noted that Hals was more likely to be in the category of those receiving home-aid.[57] (And after his death one assumes aid to his widow, who survived a number of years, continued to receive this.)

A particularly complex reading of the regentess paintings is worth quoting at length. Sheila Muller's account contrasts the "Active" and "Contemplative Life". She wants to look at the symbolic meaning relative to the sitters' actions and concludes that "there might, indeed, be evidence that, in comparison with the conventional meaning of regents group portraits in the seventeenth century, these two works have something most peculiar to say about their sitters."[58]

Muller starts with "the way in which the table which unites the sitters in the Regentessees of the Oudemannengasthuis, Haarlem is presented in full view and yet is noticeably uncluttered by the conventional items found in this location in other regents group portraits." She notes that "without these details the women, too, seem strangely unoccupied in comparison with the busy women in contemporary group portraits by Jan de Bray." Muller is working toward this point "that if charity is the work of the Active Life and it was the custom to depict this by means of objects both traditional and natural to an administrative group's good works, the conspicuous absence of these objects and the aspect of inactivity this creates strike the viewer as hinting as the opposite of virtue." She takes an objection into account. It could be said that Hals is here doing what he had done in his earlier Regents of St Elizabeth's Gathuis, that is, sparing his symbolism to let each sitter's character speak for itself through physical and mental activity. Still, she thinks "a closer look at the details that Hals does include indicates the inverse of conventional usage and symbolism, suggesting that these details are his means of commenting on character."[59]

She considers the servant: "The servant entering with a message for the regentesses is a device observed in many portraits where it is intended to give the impression that a meeting of the group is underway." But here "the bound register on the table is not open to record the event," instead, "it is shown to the viewer with its ribbon closures securely tied." Further, the regentess who is in charge of the book "makes no move to open or close it but sits looking out at the viewer with her right hand pocketed in her apron." The regentess is thus the "converse of the image of virtue as a woman working with her hands at spinning, sewing, or some other domestic chore." That converse in the seventeenth century depicted a woman "with her hands tucked into her apron to signify idleness." And then there is "an even odder evocation of the older traditions for portraying women." Muller notes that "the woman seated there at the table rests one hand on a crucifix as though claiming

---

56 Jane Turner (ed.) (2000), *Grove Dictionary of Art, Rembrandt to Vermeer* (New York: St. Martins Press), pp. 136–42 (essay on Frans Hals edited by Ingeborg Worm).

57 Sheila Muller (1985), *Charity in the Dutch Republic: Pictures of Rich and Poor for Charitable Institutions* (Ann Arbor, MI: UMI Research Press).

58 Ibid., p. 44.

59 Ibid., p. 44.

her preference—most unusual in this context—for the Contemplative Life." Finally, the treasurer, the one who sits in the treasurer's position, "has her hands spread far apart to show that there are no coins on the bare table." The conclusion is: "Within the development of the tradition behind this group portrait, the woman's gesture is tantamount to a statement—which the other figures in their own way reinforce—that there is no Active Life here."[60] And no generosity.

"As a further irony within the portrait, the painting of an Italianate landscape hanging on the wall behind the regentesses is irrelevant to both the nature of the institution and to charity." Muller's only suggestion is that it might have been the artist's intention to encourage reflection on the more general advantages of wealth, which permits the acquisition of expensive trappings such as paintings to display status as well as funding the opportunity to do good works. Her conclusion is that the use here of a painting-within-a-painting suggests to the viewer that a portrait is also a painting which, in being commissioned by the regentesses to decorate their institutional boardroom, has little to do with the true meaning of *caritas*."[61]

Alois Riegl investigates a different question, specifically the relation between certain public forms of association in Holland and the group portrait:

> The sort of corporation that the group portraiture of Holland required could only have emerged from the kind of officially incorporated groups whose members were willing to give up some of their own individuality and freedom in order to work together toward some collective, practical, secular, and public-spirited purpose. In the earliest stage of its evolution, civic guards fulfilled this requirement.[62]

He notes that: "A group portrait, as opposed to an individual portrait, unites a number of figures in one picture." Reigl's discussion of why a family portrait is not a group portrait takes us back to the legal discussions of the unity of husband and wife and the autonomy of the family considered as a unit:

> The family portrait is essentially nothing more than an elaboration of the individual portrait. A husband and a wife are, so to speak, two sides of the same coin, their children of the same stamp, and all of them are naturally of the same mintage. This family resemblance leads to a natural unity in a work of art that precludes the need for any special tricks of pictorial conception or composition.[63]

According to Riegl, the special quality of the Dutch group portraits is that:

> The groups in question consist of completely autonomous individuals who associated themselves with a corporation solely for a specific, shared, practical, and public-spirited purpose, but who otherwise wished to maintain their independence.

---

60 Ibid., p. 45.

61 Ibid., pp. 45–6.

62 Alois Riegl (1902), *The Group Portraiture in Holland*, trans. Evelyn M. Kain (Los Angeles: Getty Research Center for the History of Art and Humanities), p. 101.

63 Ibid., p. 62.

But, essentially, these group portraits are about individuals:

> At the same time, however, it is expected to express clearly the characteristics of the particular organization involved and the nature of the situation that is temporarily uniting the figures into a group. The group portrait is therefore neither an extension of individual portraiture nor a kind of mechanical arrangement of single portraits into a tableau; rather, it is the depiction of a number of autonomous members of a voluntary corporation. Another way of referring to it might be "corporate" portraiture.[64]

Riegl concludes:

> It follows that the histories of corporate organizations and of group portraiture in democratic Holland were intimately connected, and that their fortunes went hand in hand.[65]

Riegl, like others, is aware of the unseen figure in some of these group paintings, which is clearly detailed in discussing work by other painters. As to a group portrait by Van der Voort he writes: "because we know that the men in the portrait were the regents of an almshouse for old men, we can imagine the unseen party in the viewer's space as a needy elderly person (or several of them) who is seeking some form of assistance." He imagines the interaction in some detail:

> Now, four of the six men in the painting are directing their eyes toward the applicant as though asking him (or them) for the date of the last support payment. The anticipated answer is apparently a specific year, because the regent with the key to the archive is already reaching up to one of the registers, conspicuously stored up high, to select the volume with the appropriate date. The regent seated at the table has placed his left hand expectantly on his chest, as he holds a pen in his right, poised to make the necessary entry in the book lying open before him.[66]
>
> To make this figure's subordinating role clear, Valckert reverts to a time-honored device from the old civic guard group portraits by having the custodian behind the chairman point to his superior with his right hand.[67]

The power relations indicated in the painting are explored further:

> The unseen applicant is expected to respond immediately, because the second officer is already reaching for a quill and a piece of paper in order to write down the appropriate

64 Ibid., p. 62.

65 Ibid., p. 62.

66 Riegl describes a Regent's portrait by Werner van der Valckert: "First of all, however, Valckert has omitted the two debaters and has oriented all activity exclusively toward the unseen applicant. Secondly, we no longer have a doubt about who is asking the question, namely, the elderly regent on the extreme left, apparently the chairman: with his mouth still half-open, he points with his left hand toward the open book in front of him", (Ibid., p. 231).

67 Ibid., p. 223.

instructions, while the third officer has placed his finger on the stack of coins from which the relief payment will be made.[68]

(This is to be contrasted with Sheila Muller's reading of Hals work, in which there are no coins.)

A very different approach is taken by the art historian John Berger. He begins with a straightforward review of the accepted facts:

> The last two great paintings by Frans Hals portray the Governors and the Governesses of an Alms House for old paupers in the Dutch seventeenth-century city of Haarlem. They were officially commissioned portraits. Hals, an old man of over eighty, was destitute. Most of his life he had been in debt. During the winter of 1664, the year he began painting these pictures, he obtained three loads of peat on public charity, otherwise he would have frozen to death. Those who now sat for him were administrators of such public charity.[69]

Berger then turns to the work of Seymour Slive. Slive "records these facts and then explicitly says that it would be incorrect to read into the paintings any criticism of the sitters. There is no evidence, he says, that Hals painted them in a spirit of bitterness. The author considers them, however, remarkable works of art and explains why."

Berger quotes Slive's description of the Regentesses:

> Each woman speaks to us of the human condition with equal importance. Each woman stands out with equal clarity against the enormous dark surface, yet they are linked by a firm rhythmical arrangement and the subdued diagonal pattern formed by their heads and hands. Subtle modulations of the deep, glowing blacks contribute to the harmonious fusion of the whole and form an unforgettable contrast with the powerful whites and vivid flesh tones where the detached strokes reach a peak of breadth and strength.[70]

Berger summarizes his comment on Slive:

> All conflict disappears. One is left with the unchanging "human condition", and the painting considered as a marvelously made object.

It is true, Berger says, that:

> [v]ery little is known about Hals or the Regents who commissioned him. It is not possible to produce circumstantial evidence to establish what their relations were. But there is

---

68 Ibid., p. 223. The idea that the group is addressing someone outside the picture ("us, of course") is made explicit in Schama's treatment of another group portrait, Rembrandt's Staalmeesters, a picture of the men who judged the quality of cloth in Amsterdam. (Simon Schama *Rembrandt's Eyes*, (1999) (Knopf: New York) p. 649. See also treatment in Zadie Smith: "Howard looked at the men, the men looked at Howard …" Zadie Smith (2005) *On Beauty* (London/New York: Penguin) p. 383.

69 John Berger (2003[1972]), *Ways of Seeing* (London: Penguin), p. 12.

70 Ibid., p. 13 (italics omitted).

the evidence of the paintings themselves: the evidence of a group of men and a group of women as seen by another man, the painter. Study this evidence and judge for yourself.[71]

> In this confrontation the Regents and Regentesses stare at Hals, a destitute old painter who has lost his reputation and lives off public charity; he examines them through the eyes of a pauper who must nevertheless try to be objective, i.e., must try to surmount the way he sees as a pauper. This is the drama of these paintings. A drama of an "unforgettable contrast."[72]

Berger adds to the detailed descriptions of the idea that the painter is himself the petitioner. He sees Hals as "the first portraitist to paint the new characters and expressions created by capitalism."[73]

The Frans Hals portraits of those local authorities are enough to make one doubt aspects of those programs for welfare that stress the desirability of local decision making. The locals, knowing your needs, may simply be exercising a particularly well-informed kind of intimate power. The recent example of the Swiss welfare system, operating locally in a humiliating way, makes the same point.[74] The local administrators may not think particularly well of the petitioners.

As noted, the work of Frans Hals was not highly valued for several centuries, in part, perhaps, because of a view on his character. His work was considered, "lacking in finish" and this lack of finish "was associated with his dissolute way of life."[75] There is considerable discussion of whether the male regents in *The Regents of the Almshouse* are somehow drunk, echoing Hals' own reputed drunkenness.[76] Presumably the image of destitution did not help.

The outline of the life of Frans Hals suggests the connections historically between the institutions to be discussed here. It is not difficult to see the insurance company as an heir to the old guilds, and family and state are often described as if there are constants through time. A part of the argument of this book is that this is not the case. The heirs to the guilds are, of course, quite different from the guilds, not least in their abandonment of the communitarian links on which the guilds rested. (Though in the history of the trade union movement there are indications of efforts at least sometimes to reinforce communal and familial values.[77])

---

71 Ibid., p. 15.

72 Ibid., p. 15.

73 Ibid., p. 16.

74 Elizabeth Olson (2001), "In Land of Plenty, Some Swiss Struggle to Get By", including material on restitution, *New York Times*, September l, p. 13.

75 Jane Turner (ed.) *Grove Dictionary of Art*, pp. 136–42 (Essay on Frans Hals by Ingeborg Worm).

76 A good deal of Hals's bad personal reputation turns out to be attributable to the behavior of another Frans Hals who lived in Haarlem. See Michael Kernan (1994), *Lost Diary of Frans Hals* (New York: St. Martins Press) for a fictional treatment of Hals (esp. 278ff dealing with his final paintings).

77 Lizabeth Cohen (1990), *Making the Deal: Industrial Worker's Chicago* 1919–1939 (Cambridge: Cambridge University Press).

We can look at the regents and regentesses as though they represent the government. Some historians assume legitimacy and correctness in the institutions portrayed, and focus on "art" as the category for analysis. (This is John Berger's central point.) Others go more deeply into the conventional representation in Art, to reach substantive meanings (Sheila Muller's analysis, either in terms of individual character, or in terms of a political structure; Reigl's discussion of corporate life in Holland). Some people focus on the unseen beneficiary, in this case the painter, and ask about their view of the situation.

Whatever Hals thought, his view of the situation would necessarily have included the family, the guilds and the regentesses.

Pillars: Which Ones?

William Beveridge, one of the major architects of post-war Britain's welfare state, discussed the idea of pillars in two chapters in the book, *The Pillars of Security* (1943). The first discussed the pillars with a focus on domestic activity. The second treatment moved to the issue of international security.

Brian Kreisworth, commenting on Beveridge, writes:

> Like many who came after him, Beveridge sought to ensure social security through a three-pillared approach. Most importantly, he emphasized the importance of social insurance, suggesting that workers should make flat-rate contributions into a fund that would provide flat-rate, subsistence-level benefits in the event of certain widespread contingencies likely to cause need, including old age.[78]

Kreisworth stresses that Beveridge identified two other essential pillars. Beveridge wanted:

> means-tested, subsistence-level assistance for people with incomplete contribution records (although he thought this group would shrink over time); and voluntary insurance, which would contribute to the goal of income maintenance (and whose importance would be underscored by the provision of only subsistence-level state benefits, thus encouraging individuals to make private provision for retirement and other contingencies).[79]

In *The Pillars of Security*, Beveridge identified pillars and conditions of security in different ways. He referred to three conditions as "Children's allowances, paid both when the responsible parent is earning and when he is not earning … Comprehensive health and rehabilitation services for prevention and cure of disease and available to all members of the community and Maintenance of employment" (the chapter is called "Pillars of Security"). A fourth assumption was that Germany

---

78 Brian Kreiswirth (1998), "The Role of the Basic Public Pension in a Retirement Income Security System", *Comparative Labor Law and Policy Journal* 19, 393–454, p. 393.

79 Brian Kreiswirth, "The Role of the Basic Public Pension in a Retirement Income Security System", p. 407.

would be defeated in the Second World War. In the American edition of the book, a special chapter was included called "The Three Legs of Security", which picked up the theme of external security. "There are three main conditions of security in the world after the war," Beveridge wrote. It was necessary first that "justice should be established in place of force as the arbiter between nations." Second, there had to be an opportunity of productive work for every person. The third was an assurance of income sufficient to maintain someone who could not work. "Peace, a job when one can work, an income when one cannot work: Security is like a stool which will stand on three legs but falls to the ground of any of the three is missing or proves too weak …"[80]

Family and state change also over time. If the story of individual security is largely about the protection to the individual offered by these entities, it must be seen as a story that is to be told differently at different times and in different places. The point here is not that the story is the same, but that in the modern world the existence of the elements of the story is constant.

One might say that in a situation of ordinary security, the few episodes of acute insecurity are perceived as enormous, whether these relate to hurricanes or terrorism.

The contrast is to the situation that obtained through most of human history, in which ordinary life was chronically and even desperately insecure. The risks were of accident, illness and early death. The history of life expectancy of infants can be used to tell the story. It is only in this most recent past that human beings routinely expect their children to live and to be raised to adulthood. The enormous increase in life expectancy in general has to do not only with the extension of life for many people beyond 80, but also the survival of infants.

In response to this chronic insecurity, social and political institutions are developed, and two of these, the family and insurance, are the subject of this book. One cannot, after the Fall, imagine a world without a certain insecurity. The most one can do is contain or manage it in schemes that will be considered more or less utopian, depending on who is doing the evaluating.

Our own visions are more typically more secular and more optimistic. Despair is not the motif. If we are, as one might say, desperately seeking security, we are involved in an active search. It may be, however, as another line has it, that we are looking in the wrong places. The message of the Brecht/Weill opera, *The Rise and Fall of the City of Mahogonny* is that there is nothing on which man can rely.[81] But even if this is true, ultimately, finally, it may be useful to think about the particular

---

80 William Beveridge (1943), *The Pillars of Security* (New York: Macmillan), p. 221.

81 Berthold Brecht (1996[1927]), *The Rise and Fall of the City of Mahagonny and The Seven Deadly Sins* (trans. W.H. Auden and Chester Kallman) (New York: Arcade Publishing)."Why, though, did we need a Mahagonny?/Because this world is a foul one/With neither charity/Nor peace nor concord/Because there's nothing to build any trust upon" (p. 64).

ways in which we, in a certain time and place, can and cannot rely on specific institutions.

But while part of the argument about mechanisms for security is about support for those in need, those whose deprivation is pronounced, beneath the level at which others can simply walk away, another part of the argument is about protection from diminution in holdings or status. And here there is a problem since fluctuation is a part of a normal market situation. Other institutions will have to protect stability and the current state. When? And how?

As to the poor, the public almshouse, which figures in the account of American treatments of the poor,[82] was considered an unsuitable remedy by the time of the New Deal. The Social Security Act provided that money would not be available for those who lived in public institutions.

And we often talk as though people who received aid, or lived in almshouses were passive, among the disappeared, or the non-existing, people without agency or impact. But the Frans Hals painting is a particularly clear indication that this is not true. Those receiving aid look back at those who are giving it, in the role of governors and overseers.

The sophisticated versions of that idea of the individual in society move on to describe institutions, the state, for example, or the family. They might also describe particular economic structures, the non-profit corporation, or the profit or non-profit insurance company. The state itself may be described in terms of mutual aid ideas, since the state is supposed to take care, as inheritor of that protective role of the prince.

The premise of this book is that government has a major role in providing security, and that most modern Western governments do so in a variety of ways. The methods include direct financial benefits and pensions. But the government assessments rely on other institutions. First among these is the family, which has historically been associated with the state, and which has traditionally been linked to property. A second is insurance.

Further, the "state," while a word used by many states, is in fact quite specific in its meaning in any given state. One can reach this through political theory or iconography. French books on the welfare state by Pierre Rosanvallon and Francois Ewald[83] both use a cover reproducing Daumier's painting *La Republique.* We are told that:

> Daumier conceived the Republic as the protecting and guiding mother of the people. Posed against a plain, neutral background, an impassive but inspiring figure with sinewy muscles, she sits upon a squarely constructed throne and gathers in one hand the folds of

82 See for example Abraham Epstein (1936), *Insecurity; A Challenge to America* (New York: Random House), pp. 507 ff.

83 Pierre Rosanvallon (1998), *La Nouvelle Question Sociale: Repenser l'Etat Providence* (The new social question: Rethinking the welfare state) (Editions du Seuil); Francois Ewald (1996), *Histoire de, L'Etat Providence: Les Origines de La Solidarité* (History of the welfare state: The origins of solidarity) (Grasset).

> the tricolor as she holds the staff like a scepter. Two unclothed children standing close at her side take nourishment from her great breasts, while a third, seated at her feet and reading a book, signifies the educational function of the State, and thus carries out the complete title given to the picture: La République nourrit ses enfants et les instruit. The departures from the letter of the program were accepted by the jury, as if the children's figures were to be considered merely as attributes.[84]

In 1850, Frederic Bastiat used and rejected the same image: "The law is not a breast that fills itself with milk." The money given to the poor would be plundered from someone else.[85]

This debate is still alive, as is the debate over the moral worthiness of the poor, the idea of harm as a consequence of divine judgment, and the issue of the proper role and shape of the family. It is the family that is the subject of Chapter 2.

---

84 Bernard Lemann (1945), "Daumier and the Republic", *Gazette des beaux-arts*, 27:6, 105–20.

85 Frederic Bastiat (1990), *The Law* (trans. Dean Russell) (Irvington-on-Hudson, NY: Foundation for Economic Education), p. 31.

Chapter 2

Security through the Family

> The long and short of this dependence upon family solidarity is just this: (1) That in a number of cases the aged poor are single individuals, (2) Or if married or widowed, have no children, (3) And if there are adult children or other relatives they are unable to render any aid, or, at any rate, sufficient aid, (4) Or if they are able, may not be willing to do so.
>
> I.M. Rubinow[1]

As Rubinow's comment indicates, the traditional entry into discussions of family security is marriage. In effect, he says this: "We talk about family support and solidarity but there may be those who are single, having no families because they never married or married without children. Or they may have children but no support, having families but not families capable of providing support. Marriage is the center of the analysis."

We are directed then to consider the family and security and the subject "marriage and security," at least as a point of entry. What are we, now in the early twenty-first century in the United States, talking about, when we talk about marriage?

We can start with the traditional ideas:

> Marriage, while from its very nature a sacred obligation, is nevertheless, in most civilized nations, a civil contract, and usually regulated by law. Upon it society may be said to be built, and out of its fruits spring social relations and social obligations and duties, with which government is necessarily required to deal.[2]

This language, from *Reynolds v. United States*, the Mormon polygamy case of 1879, remained foundational in the law of the family and in the social understanding until very recently.

It is language that has been quoted many times. Yet it has some odd aspects and qualifications. Marriage is a sacred obligation but also "in most civilized nations" a civil contract. In Catholic doctrine, marriage was a sacrament, and it was Protestant nations that conceived marriage as a civil contract. And thus "most civilized nations," means that some nations are not among these, and "usually regulated by law," meaning that some places—Mormon Utah, for example—that had no law of marriage, were not to be taken into account.

1 I.M. Rubinow (1913), *Social Insurance* (New York: Henry Holt), p. 315.

2 *Reynolds v. United States*, 98 US 145 (1879).

The language from *Reynolds* was as important as the earlier language from the English (also Mormon) case *Hyde v. Hyde*.[3] Marriage was one man, one woman for life to the exclusion of all others. The formula of *Hyde* as it included "for life" was eroded by the end of the nineteenth century as looser divorce laws undercut the binding character of the institution. By the time of this writing, it is the man–woman part of the definition that is heavily under attack.

And the language of *Reynolds*, insisting on the foundational nature of marriage for the state itself, seems no longer as descriptive as it once was. Marriage may not be the foundation of the state. Marriage pretty clearly is not as important as it once was. Significantly, a casebook which for two of its three editions began with material on the importance of marriage, in its third edition changed the heading to the Importance of the Family.[4] But while it is striking that writers have for some time questioned whether marriage was necessary for the state,[5] it seems more significant that the Supreme Court of the United States, in dealing with the issue of grandparents visiting the children of an unmarried couple, dealt casually with the fact that here was no marriage, without attributing any particular significance to it.[6] The marital status of the biological parents had become essentially irrelevant to the questions under discussion. In fact, we can describe the revolutionary changes[7] by a contrast between two cases, one decided in 1967, the other in 2000. Both cases are about grandparents, parents and children. The grandparents in the later litigation were only two among the several sets of grandparents. The marital group was the biological mother and her (new) husband. Where the parents in the first case were married, the parents in the second case were not and the matter is not even discussed.

Painter v. Bannister (1966)[8] involved a widower who lost custody to his wife's parents. The case is understood either in terms of a court finding for conventional grandparents over the claims of a fit but unconventional father, or as a case heavily influenced by a psychologist's testimony on the child's need for continuity.[9] In 1967, the case would have looked entirely different if the bohemian actor had been an unwed father. In May 2000, the Supreme Court of the United States decided that parents had the right to decide visitation issues relating to their children and that even grandparents were subject to that decision. The *Troxel*[10] grandparents (parents

3 *Hyde v. Hyde*, L.R. 1 P&D 130 (1866).

4 L. Harris, L. Teitelbaum and J. Carbone (2005), *Family Law*, 3rd edn. (New York: Aspen).

5 For example, Martha Fineman (2001), "Why Marriage?", *Virginia Journal of Social Policy and the Law* 9, 239–71.

6 Contrast the approach of a collection of essays compiled by the Association of American Law Schools which used as a heading in the table of contents "The Incomplete Family of the Illegitimate Child." *Selected Essays on Family Law*, AALS (1950) (Brooklyn: Foundation Press).

7 Other changes in family law, equally revolutionary, are outlined in Lee Teitelbaum (1996), "The Last Decades of American Family Law", *Journal of Legal Education* 546.

8 *Painter v. Bannister*, 140 N.W. 2d 152 (Iowa) (1966).

9 For an expanded discussion see Weisbrod (2006) *Painter v Bannister*: Still, 2006 *Utah Law Review*, 135–156.

10 *Troxel v. Granville*, 530 US 57 (2000).

of a deceased son) began their legal battle with a struggle for increased access to a grandchild through a claim to visitation more extensive than the parent would allow. The Supreme Court of the United States accepted the case, upheld the right of the mother—the biological parent—and her new spouse, to the determining weight in visitation question.

Grandparents are important in both cases. But do we know how to think about them? Two images of grandparents are caught in *New York Times* stories published in July 2005. One is about the contributions that wealthy grandparents, those described as "financially set" make to support the upper-middle-class lifestyle of their children and grandchildren, who are unable to sustain such a life without assistance.[11] (In the background is the familiar story about another part of the culture, in which grandmothers of minority groups take care of the grandchildren.) Another concerns the middle-class grandparents, struggling with the rules of American Medicaid, state assistance for those who cannot afford long-term nursing home care on their own. This article focuses on the problems of those grandparents who are running out of money at the end of their lives.[12] In one story, the grandparents share their security; in the second, they impose their insecurity. Do we know the general story about families and security of which these pictures are snapshots?

Family and Property

While it is widely understood that families provide security, and that this is indeed one of the major functions of the family, some research on security-providing institutions brackets discussion of the family. Even, for example, work that stresses the significance of non-government programs (see, for example, Jacob Hacker's recent scholarship[13]) does not deal with the family. While also noting the significance of "transfers" within families, Hacker classifies family support as private, but also as almost altogether free of governmental influence.[14] This point, of course, could be presented differently. In the same way that many other "private" security programs are shaped by government, the family is also. Moreover, much of what the family provides may not be captured by the idea of "transfer". While certainly wealth transfer takes place, even transfer in measurable dollar amounts, this is clearly not the limit of what the family provides. Similarly, meeting support obligations can be classified as "informal"[15] though there is in the background a legal dimension. The analytic

11 Tamar Lewin (2005), "Financially set, grandparents help keep families afloat", *New York Times*, July 14, Section A, col, 1, p. 1.

12 Jane Gross (2005), "The Middle Class Struggles in the Medicaid Maze", *New York Times*, July 9, Section B, col. 2, p. 1.

13 Jacob Hacker (2002), *The Divided Welfare State* (Cambridge: Cambridge University Press).

14 He acknowledges that some would do this differently.

15 See Norman Stein "Retirement Planning", in W.J. Turnier and G.M.P McCouch (eds), *Family Wealth Management* (St. Paul, MN: Thomson/West), pp. 565–65, p. 572. What is

problem here is that the fact that individuals comply with a legal and social norm does not mean that these obligations are "informal". Moreover, the legal and social norm relate to each other, the legal norm (for example relating to the support obligations of marriage) often heavily dependent on the social norm, while also shaping it.[16]

Part of the weakness of the current discussion is probably best described in terms of an old joke. One looks for the lost item under the lamppost not because it was lost there but because that is where the light is. When transactions can be described as dollar transfers and then quantified, those writers most comfortable with material presented in these categories are satisfied. Those who stress subjective and intangible aspects of family support may be less satisfied. This point comes up regularly in general with reference to law and economics scholarship, which excludes many things as beyond the questions the discipline can engage.[17]

A large focus of the history of the law of the family was once property.[18] This is evident in Pollock and Maitland. The theme is also pursued in the work of Julius Goebel, who remarked that "as Karl Marx very clearly noticed, there has always been an interdependence of family and property." When, in 1946, Goebel included a section on family law in his *Cases and Materials on the Development of Legal Institutions*,[19] he produced a table of contents that reads—at least in the section on the common law and the family—like the outline of the first semester of a standard property course.

But this merges two points that might well be separated. First, that the law of the family has a close connection to the law of property. Second, that the family as a social institution has a great deal to do with property and thus security and that this social institution is not entirely defined by law.

As to the first, the links between the law of the family and the law of property surprise us. This is so because in recent memory family law was often focused on conflicts of laws and, later, on issues of psychology and the integration of this field

---

meant here is presumably that most support obligations in the family do not require court orders (though some do, most obviously when there is family breakdown). As to the limit, see *McGuire v. McGuire*, 59 NW 2d 336 (Neb. 1953).

16 Martha Minow (1992–93), "All in the Family and in All Families Loving and Owing", *West Virginia Law Review* 95, 275–332. See discussion in Frances E. Olsen (1985), "The Myth of State Intervention in the Family", *University of Michigan Journal of Law Reform* 18, 835–64.

17 See, for example, the discussion of method in the material on guaranteed income, and particularly the criticisms to the effect that noting an increase in divorce where there was an assured income said nothing at all about whether this increase was good or bad. Alicia Munnell (ed.) (1986), *Lesson from the Income Maintenance Experiments* (Boston, MA: Federal Reserve Bank of Boston and the Brookings Institution).

18 This discussion draws on Carol Weisbrod (2000), "A Comment on Property and Divorce", *Connecticut Law Review* 32, 291–8; Weisbrod (2000), "*Kirksey v. Kirksey*: An Uncertain Trumpet", *Connecticut Law Review* 32, 291–298.

19 Julius Goebel (1946), *Cases and Materials on the Development of Legal Institutions* (Brattelboro, VT: Vermont Publishing).

with the social sciences. Leading examples of such writings have, for example, focused on the welfare of children using social science perspectives. More recently, under the impact of feminist theory, family law and constitutional law came closer together. As to the second, the links surprise us because we have been so focused on the psychological and emotional aspects of marriage and the family (though perhaps issues of family wealth are re-emerging as Elder Law, for example, becoming obviously more significant) that we have only recently rediscovered its economic functions.[20]

The issues of security and the family affect everyone, since everyone is first an infant and, if all goes well, a senior citizen. But perhaps one must note that issues of security and the family relate in a very intense way to the situation of women. One might say that it has been conventional for decades that the subject of family law is of special concern to women. But where family law once meant something about a description of the condition of women—a description written largely by men relatively satisfied with what they saw—to the extent that it deals with women now, it more and more opens questions about structural tensions between the family and the outside environment.[21] These feminist questions are as radical as those traditionally posed by Marxist and Utopian thinkers.

I.M. Rubinow saw the normal pattern. For most of Western history, the dominant career for women was marriage, and that economic self-sufficiency for women was an extremely rare thing:

> So long as this normal pattern remains undisturbed—father–mother–children–job—there is a normal pattern of life. It may be on any one of the numerous steps of the economic ladder; but the family has a normal grip on life. It is not swinging in the air, so to speak, with one hand holding onto the ladder and frantically trying to find a footing.[22]

Rubinow thought that the old agricultural family, in its multigenerational and patriarchal form, was dead. (His use of the term patriarchal referred, it seems, a family headed by a grandfather rather than a male-dominated couple.)

By now, it is clear that some of this normal pattern is dramatically changed. No-fault divorce changed the family in quite a fundamental way. The conventional understandings about the fault system, in which a wife would allow a divorce, and would sue her husband for divorce in a system that was to appear adversarial, rested on a bargain. She would give him "his freedom" in return for a decent settlement and custody of the children. When no-fault eliminated her power to withhold the divorce, her power to bargain for her own security was correspondingly reduced.

---

20 See discussion in Weisbrod, "*Painter v. Bannister*: Still".

21 See, for example, a recent discussion comparing situation of American and French women. The suggestion here is that earlier in America, there was considerable social support for mothering which has now been lost. Judith Warner (2005), *Perfect Madness* (New York: Riverside).

22 I.M. Rubinow (1934), *The Quest for Security* (New York: Henry Holt), p. 17.

This is what, in the United States, produced what is called the new impoverishment of women and children.[23]

Arguments over the appropriate role of the divorced husband in the support of his wife continue. Rehabilitative alimony ideas suggest that she should, under the correct circumstances, be permitted only enough to become self-supporting. Property settlements, which may be based on equality/community ideas in general, become complicated when we see the CEO (Chief Executive Officer) divorce, in which no matter how handsome the settlement for the wife, it will not equal a half interest in the property of the CEO.[24]

Some public entitlements for women turn on their marital status (for example, social security benefits for widows). Others involve entitlements that the women has as an individual. But to the extent that programs rest on the assumption that there is a family in the background in most cases (and, as a Justice of the Supreme Court once said, the law concerns itself with the generality of things and not with exceptions)[25] the shape of that family matters. We must know whether it is in fact able to provide for the security of women, whether the governmental entitlement is conceived as a supplement or as a basic and even substantial entitlement to an individual whose claim is made individually and not through a connection to a male wage earner.

Maitland said that when we link probate and divorce it is because we remember the courts Christian, whose jurisdiction included both. But we also link probate and divorce because of our sense that security in old age or disability rests on both money and people, and that the family was associated with both.

But dynastic wealth transmission through the family has changed, as John Langbein has demonstrated.[26] More may be above inter-vivos. But with a high divorce rate, this has its own risks.

The shape of the family has changed and includes different people at different times. To the extent that security through financial support is a concern of the law, it shows up directly in the area of divorce and custody of small children, and here we see the American Law Institute, for example, trying to sort out such questions as the support obligation of parents by estoppel (some of whom may be prevented from denying that they are parents at all) and the obligations of parents (however created)

---

23 See particularly the work of Lenore Weitzman on the marriage contract and on the impact of divorce; Lenore Weitzman (1983), *The Marriage Contract* (New York: Free Press).

24 See Joan Williams and Gallivan Conference (2000), "Do Wives Own Half? Winning for Wives after Wendt", *Connecticut Law Review* 32, 249-80.

25 *Bradwell v. State*, 83 US 130 (1872), Bradley concurrence, joined by Justices Swayne and Field: "It is true that many women are unmarried and not affected by any of the duties, complications and incapacities arising out of the married state, but these are exceptions to the general rule. The paramount destiny and mission of woman are to fulfill the noble and benign offices of wife and mother. This is the law of the Creator. And the rules of civil society must be adapted to the general constitution of things, and cannot be based upon exceptional cases."

26 John Langbein (1988), "The Twentieth-Century Revolution in Family Wealth Transmission", *Michigan Law Review* 86, 722–51.

to adult children who are once again, through illness for example, dependent.[27] It is not that it is impossible to sort out such obligations. It is more that the idea that if we have to do so, if a court must intervene and issue an order to establish the regime of support, all of this is contrary to the matter of fact assumption that is implied in the idea of the traditional family that one will be taken care of.

And we should not take the shape for granted—Rubinow made the point about shape. "Another matter which has a much greater practical importance than would appear at first glance is the compensation right of brothers and sisters," he wrote. "Singularly enough their rights are quite universally disregarded. Only in Italy and Russia are their rights provided for, of course following those of immediate family and dependent parents. Yet it is quite usual for a younger person to contribute to the family budget, and a more direct support of younger brothers and sisters is a matter of common occurrence in the wage-worker's life." This was an important issue, he thought, since over one-third of the fatal accidents occur to unmarried workmen, and since parents are only entitled to compensation when their dependency is established, many minor brothers and sisters are unjustly deprived of their means of support."[28]

If, in general, the fields of property and family law are closer than one might think at first, there are also significant differences. One difference is around the time frame. Family law is often focused on crisis intervention, picking up the pieces of an immediate and even urgent problem. When it takes a long view, it is often a view backwards, as when we ask whether, decades after the event, some marriage should be annulled, or whether some child was, in childhood, abused so that, perhaps, they should not have to support an elderly parent.

Property, by contrast, is often associated with a long view forward, with the control of the dead hand, for example, into the remote future. The rule against perpetuities is itself indicative of the desire to control the future. And the language of property often evokes the continuities of the field: ancestral lands, dynastic wealth. The language of family law, particularly to the extent that it is about love and affection, is focused on emotion to such a degree that the specific question is raised whether emotion should or could be the source of obligation.[29]

---

27 American Law Institute (2002), *Principles of the Law of Family Dissolution* (Newark, NJ: H. Bender), 3.24, c.g.

28 Rubinow, *Social Insurance*, p. 126.

29 A question as to alimony and also support of parents. Family is thought to provide present and future security for wife and elderly parents. It's also the source of security for children while small and of future security to the extent that this can be protected. While the very rich protect the security of their children with trust funds, others will invest in their children's human capital, assuming that expensive education and professional training will provide security and more. This may be correlated to class and ideology, as Christopher Lasch pointed out in his account of the American abortion controversy. The elites will stress family planning and heavy investment in each child, attempting by rational choices and deliberate success strategies to get a deliberately limited number of children to the top. The working class may assume that there is a limit to what one can achieve by oneself that the world is not so susceptible to engineering and manipulation , and that the future will come and will take

Stressing the long view, we often teach property beginning with feudalism, one of the conditions—for example, barbarism, tribalism, and, recently, liberalism—in which people are said to be "mired". And, recalling what we once knew about feudal estates, we remember such forms as to "A and the Heirs of his Body."

What mechanisms are left to protect property of either family or group in age of equitable distribution on divorce? In some versions of the distributions, states will protect a "separate property" if it remains separate. Thus we are told: separate property may become marital property.[30] If, for example, one spouse receives a gift of money during marriage from a parent and deposits it into a bank account where they also deposits their earnings, the gift will likely become hopelessly mixed, or "commingled" with marital assets and, as a result, be treated as marital property. Or, if the money is deposited in a joint account, in many states a presumption will arise that the owner intended to make a gift to the marital estate and the funds will be "transmuted" from separate to marital property.[31]

In any case, in some states, any property acquired during marriage from any source will be available for distribution. (Contractual arrangements are possible of course.)

This is more than an issue for the very rich. Many people want to give money, particular things, whether or not of extrinsic value, within the bloodline or within the group. Simes writes: "It must not be supposed that the future interest and the rules of law which restrict it can be understood outside its natural setting. That setting is the family settlement, the dispositions, whether by will or inter vivos, by which the man of property attempts to tie up his estate in the family."[32] While the recent changes in family wealth transmission focus on the inter-vivos transaction,[33] we seem not to have focused in the way in which those inter-vivos transactions may have changed in response to divorce and the new approaches to economic arrangements after divorce. Anecdotal material suggests that older generations are aware of the instabilities in the lives of younger ones.

The field of property contains various narratives. Some involve the story of free alienation of land, which we could re-open in terms of individualism to pick up the strands often deprecated under the name "dead hand law", which stressed family, groups and continuities.

What it does not stress, however, is the security of individuals. The dead hand limits the rights of individuals, sometimes historically in the context of illegitimacy,

---

care of itself. Thus Lasch writes: "The debate about abortion illustrates the difference between the enlightened ethic of competitive achievement and the petty bourgeouise or working class ethic of limits". Christopher Lasch (1991), *The True and only Heaven: Progress and its Critics*. (New York: Norton), p. 489.

30 H. Kraus et al. (1998), *Family Law*, 4th edn. (St Paul, MN: West Group), p. 728.

31 Ibid.

32 From Lewis Simes (1966), *Handbook on Future Interests*, 2nd edition. (St Paul, MN: West Publishing), p. 3.

33 See Langbein, "The Twentieth-Century Revolution in Family Wealth Transmission", p. 2.

most obviously now in the possibility of inheritance. The nuclear family may be about the security of infant babies. It seems not, however, to be concerned with the lifelong security of those who were infants. And the nuclear family, in our time, is a form, a mold, into which from time-to-time different individuals are placed, or place themselves, for a particular period of time. It is as if the traditional family existed in time, while the current family exists in space.

Home is the place where when you go there, they have to take you in. This, like the idea that childhood is the kingdom where nobody dies, is now and probably always was counterfactual. But in our world the facts have changed so thoroughly that it seems quixotic to rely on the family, and particularly on the marital family, as the source of continuing and permanent security that will be sufficient to sustain an individual throughout life and particularly an increasingly long life. After describing the family as a kind of insurance institution, Robert Shiller notes that the family has serious limitations in this regard. It is "too small and unstable a group to be reliable." He details the point this way: "family members may die or move away or they may become irresponsible." Relations within a family can and often do break down, leading to an atmosphere that can be deeply depressing and even destructive. In the United States and many other countries, roughly half of all marriages end in divorce. While the family can assist in a crisis and sometimes operate to keep a family together, it is also true that "reliance on the economic function of the family can keep some people in terrible marriages for decades."[34] Ellman's "Theory of Alimony" raises the problem in the context of support after divorce:

> None of this denies that many divorced women confront difficult financial circumstances, but the financial need of one spouse at the termination of a marriage does not lead inevitably to the conclusion that the other spouse must meet that need. A theory of alimony must explain why spouses should be liable for each other's needs after their marriage has ended. Why should the needy person's former spouse provide support rather than his parents, his children, or society as a whole?[35]

The idea that the work of government ought to be grounded empirically is not new, but it is not -still- descriptive of the way governments work.[36] We are still debating these questions as a matter of policy or morality, with little empirical grounding.

---

34 Robert Shiller, *The New Financial Order: Risk in the 21st Century* (Princeton, NJ and Oxford: Princeton University Press), p. 41. Ira Ellman (1989), "Theory of Alimony", *California Law Review* 77, 1–62. Christopher Lasch, *The True and only Heaven*, p. 489.

35 Ellman, "Theory of Alimony".

36 Not only are there no underpinnings empirically, but even when there are assertions of such underpinnings—as in recent statement that children are best off in two parent families—it seems that the data is often read ideologically. For example, the two parent family is juxtaposed with one parent with serious problems. This ignores the point that the term "single mother" covers many kinds of mothers, divorced, widowed, never married, wage earner, professional, impoverished.

The economic perspective today resonates with that of an earlier period. Thus, Gary Becker, in his Nobel Lecture, recently argued that "parents who do not need support when they become old do not try as hard to make children more loyal or guiltier or otherwise feel as well disposed to their parents." The conclusion was that "programs such as social security that significantly help the elderly would encourage family members to drift apart, emotionally, not by accident but as maximizing responses to those policies."[37] Rubinow, in 1936,[38] quoted an economist for the state of Massachusetts to the effect that non-contributory programs to support the elderly would weaken family solidarity.

As to the empirical claims in Becker's argument, it is hard to think that this reflects universal experience. Similarly, one wonders about the empirical validity of the idea that threats of disinheritance are not credible.[39] If we all construct the world we say we are describing, perhaps it would make sense to concede that there may be descriptions that were constructed differently, perhaps out of different raw materials.

It may be noted that these comments on description are linked to arguments on the need for serious empirical work in family law.[40] Lee Teitelbaum, for example, was concerned particularly about ideologically driven predictions of the results of certain legal changes. Law and economics as much as any other field predicts based on assumptions about human behavior. But the point holds also for the description of the reality which the change is intended to influence. Much of our writing assumes that the nuclear family exists alone, or perhaps in a community, but downplays the significance of the grandparent generation, for example. When we say that husband and wife decide things—Teitelbaum, for example, illustrates with husband and wife deciding who works and who stays home—we ignore not only the powerful influences of the peer culture but also the intense pressures of families of origin.[41]

The impact of divorce on the security of the wife particularly in the nuclear family has been much discussed. Less discussed by the academics but possibly visible in the practices of family and trusts and estates lawyers, is the impact of divorce on the behavior of the grandparent generation. Are they waiting to give large amounts of

37 Gary Becker (1993), "Nobel lecture: 'The Economic Way of Looking at Behaviour'", *Journal of Political Economy* 101, 385–409.

38 Rubinow, *The Quest for Security*, p. 251. he refers to this report again (and quotes it) at p. 267.

39 See Margaret Brinig (1996), "The Family Franchise: Elderley Parents and Adult Siblings", *Utah Law Review* 393–428.

40 See Lee Teitelbaum (1985), "An Overview of Law and Social Research" *Journal of Legal Education* 35, 465–77; (1999) "Rays of Light", *Journal of Law and Family Studies* 1, 1–12.

41 Of course this is different in different religious and ethnic groups. It may become visible to the couples themselves largely through intermarriage. See the discussion in Harvey Cox (2001), *Common Prayers* (Boston, MA: Houghton Mifflin), of the familism of his Jewish wife, surprising to him since his family assumed that after a certain age you were pretty much on your own. I am indebted to the late Rev. Nanette E. Geertz for this reference.

money to the couple until the marriages in effect vests, perhaps at the birth of the first child? Are they skipping a generation and giving gifts or setting up trusts directly for the child? Are they using up their assets (as suggested by John Langbein) and spending down, so that they will be eligible for public programs, having transferred their wealth, large or small, inter-vivos? Are they defining their support role more as creating human capital than in transferring their wealth at death? Have matters proceeded beyond Langbein, so that people are so afraid of an impoverished old age that they are not even investing in human capital for others but are saving for their own old age? Do people expect their children to pay for graduate school (parents having paid for college)? Do they expect their children to get loans and pay for college on their own?

From the point of view of individuals, the difficulty is that the mechanisms through which we provide security are themselves unreliable. Government policies change as governments change, statutes can be repealed, and constitutional understandings can be revised. Insurance policies are cancelled, and for one reason or another made unavailable to the insured. And families are not it seems the source of security that they were once thought to be.[42]

Even the idea of the family as a place where one is cared for becomes complicated for us. James Wilson wants to define caretaking as one on one.[43] But does that mean that people who hire people to be the one on one, in whole or part, have failed in their duties as caretakers?[44]

Negative images of the family are common. The family is the site of particularism, the teacher of injustice[45] and in general a hot house of intense and even violent emotion. Hannah Arendt describes the "security of darkness" in the private realm of family life.[46] Our sense is that that darkness and family privacy can be quite damaging.

That is not, however, the subject here, nor is it the central point. Rather, the point is that while there are some things that the family does uniquely—and particularly those things dealing with emotion—there are other things, having to do with long-term security for example, which it does but possibly does badly. Other institutional forms may do better, at any rate, in principle more universally and more rationally. An unjust leader, king or president would replicate the injustice in the family. It is no accident that patriarchal forms exist in both family and government. But the

42 To what extent, and for whom, they once were is an entirely different issue.

43 James Q. Wilson, (2002) *The Marriage Problem* (New York: HarperCollins).

44 *Borelli v. Brusseau*, 16 California Reptorter 2d 16 (Cal /App 1993), discussed in Nancy Cott, (2000) *Public Vows: The History of Marriage and the Nation* (Cambridge: Harvard University Press). See in general Brian Bix (2004), "Public and Private Ordering of Marriage", in *Chicago Legal Forum*, 295–318.

45 See Carol Weisbrod, (1999) *Butterfly, the Bride* (Ann Arbor, MI: University of Michigan Press), pp. 73–93.

46 Hannah Arendt (1968[1961], "Crisis in Education", in *Between Past and Present* (New York: The Viking Press), pp. 173-96. p. 186.

intensity of dispute in small units is well known.[47] It would seem that larger social groups would be more able to rise above—or perhaps it is below—the intense and volatile world of intimate relationships. The family plays a critical role, in its allocation decisions, in shaping individual life. At the level of lifelong security, other institutions have an equally critical role in protecting individuals as part of the social fabric.

The Impact of Contract Law

The civil obligations of marriage included a support obligation of the husband towards the wife (now reciprocal) as well as support obligations towards children and sometimes other relatives, under relative responsibility law derived from the Elizabethan poor law. As noted above, the earlier world of the family included the extended family in ways that implicate issues of security.

Kirksey v. Kirksey[48] contains one of the several memorable pieces of family correspondence in the first-year contracts class in American law schools. The critical letter reads as follows:

> Dear sister Antillico–Much to my mortification, I heard, that brother Henry was dead, and one of his children. I know that your situation is one of grief, and difficulty. You had a bad chance before, but a great deal worse now. I should like to come and see you, but cannot with convenience at present.
>
> I do not know whether you have a preference on the place you live on, or not. If you had, I would advise you to obtain your preference, sell the land, and quit the country, as I understand it is very unhealthy, and I know society is very bad. If you will come down and see me, I will let you have a place to raise your family, and I have more open land than I can tend; and on the account of your situation, and that of your family, I feel like I want you and the children to do well.

The court's opinion in the case is very brief and can be given here in full.

> ORMOND, J.– "The inclination of my mind, is, that the loss and inconvenience, which the plaintiff sustained in breaking up, and moving to the defendant's, a distance of sixty miles, is a sufficient consideration to support the promise, to furnish her with a house, and land to cultivate, until she could raise her family. My brothers, however, think that the promise on the part of the defendant was a mere gratuity and that an action will not lie for its breach. The judgment of the Court below must therefore be reversed, pursuant to the agreement of the parties."[49]

---

47 Zechariah Chafee (1930), "Internal Affairs of Associations Not for Profit", *Harvard Law Review* 43, 993–1030.

48 This draws on Weisbrod, "*Kirksey v. Kirksey*: An Uncertain Trumpet".

49 *Kirksey v. Kirksey*, 8 Ala 131 (1845).

This is not the sort of opinion that one can treat at length, analyzing the intricacies of argument.[50] Indeed, the reference to the inclination of a judge's mind suggests that argument and analysis may not even be the foundation of the judgment. Nonetheless the opinion is of interest. Of its 98 words, 52 are given to a description of the conclusion of the dissenting judge, the writer of the opinion. The "holding" is given as a conclusion, in 27 words. This action will not lie. No cases are cited, from Alabama or any other jurisdiction. Like many contracts cases, *Kirksey v. Kirksey* is short. The opinion by John J. Ormond, is shorter than the document containing the promise in litigation.

Like *Mills v. Wyman*,[51] Kirksey could easily be used as a probe into life in Alabama in 1845. We have a widow, her brother-in-law, and her sons. The letter recites what seems, as a preliminary matter, to be an odd circumstance. A brother does not seem to know of his brother's death. Other matters are equally ambiguous. What do we know about the children? Why did the widow simply abandon her land? Under what arrangement did she hold it? What does the $200 that she was given by the jury represent? (Her moving expenses? Wages for her work on the land for the time she was on the land?) What does the letter mean when it says "to raise your family"? Perhaps, two years later, she actually had raised her family, on some standard or other. (Was it possible to argue that the promise had in fact been fully performed?) Was there some sense of an underlying obligation to his brother's widow?[52]

One can look at any case in a broader context than the doctrinal one in which it is presented in a law school casebook.[53] In the first-year course, cases that are obvious candidates for people interested in family law, for example, are *Strong v. Sheffield*, which could be considered against the background of married women's property acts and the issue of married women as sureties for their husbands (an issue that is still alive); or *Mills v. Wyman* against the background of the early American poor laws; or *Brackenbury v. Hodgkin*, as a problem in Elder law.[54] *Kirksey v. Kirksey* might, along

---

50 For an example of this sort of analysis, see Leon Lipson (1977), "The Allegheny College Case", *Yale Law Report* 23, 8–11.

51 See Geofrey Watson (1997),"In the Tribunal of Conscience: Mills v. Wyman", *Tulane Law Journal*, 800, 1744–1806, p. 1749. The case is discussed in Chapter 4 below.

52 If we say that popular culture disseminates legal norms, isn't it also possible that the emphasis on biblical material in the nineteenth century, with constant exposure to the text of the King James Bible, preserved some version of the norms of levirate marriage? The Jewish Law obligation, focused on a man dying childless, can show up in state laws that enforce religious law. See, for example, the law of pre-revolutionary Russia, quoted by Hyacinthe Ringrose (1988[1910], *Law of Marriage and Divorce*. (Littleton, CO: Rothman). If a woman's husband has died childless, and is survived by a brother, she can marry no one else than this brother until the latter has declined marriage with her in the prescribed form. Cf. Deuteronomy, Chapter 25, 5–9.

53 See, for example, Mary Jo Frug's discussion of *Parker v. 20th Century Fox* in relation to feminist issues, Mary Jo Frug (1985), "Rereading Contracts", *Cal Reptr* 737, 1065–140.

54 *Strong v. Sheffield*, 144 NY 392 (1895); *Mills v. Wyman*, 3 Pick 207 Mass (1825); *Brackenbury v. Hodgkin*, 102 A. 106 (1917).

these lines, be considered with reference to the issues of relative responsibility laws, or even the penumbral obligations of marriage. *Kirksey* raises issues of the extended family and moral obligation, which sometimes are litigated as legal obligation.

From the opinion, we know very little about the breakdown in relations. But if the opinion had recited facts, we would have reason to be suspicious of them in any case.[55] Perhaps Sister Antillico was impossible to live with. Perhaps her brother-in-law was more and more difficult and demanding, even inappropriately demanding. Someone presumably knew once, perhaps even the judges. We don't know. At the same time, the outline of the facts seems plain. A man writes to his brother's widow suggesting that she should come and live with him. He does not suggest anything directly by way of exchange. He does not say "to be my housekeeper/mistress/hired hand" or anything else that might suggest that he could derive some benefit from the exchange. Nor does he even say that he individually and personally wants intensely to see her. The rules of contracts on such matters are thought to be plain. Or to have been plain. A promise must be supported by consideration. Family promises are no different in this respect from any other. Reliance alone, when unbargained for, will not support a promise. Was the promise to Sister Antillico part of an exchange or was it simply a gratuity?

It is on this point that the case was of interest to Samuel Williston,[56] who included it in his casebook on Contracts. Williston concluded that the result of the case was unjust, and said so, in comments on the Restatement of Contracts.[57] Corbin was also interested in the case, asking in his treatment whether section 90 of the Restatement, the promissory estoppel section, might have been useful and whether one wanted to think about the value of her reliance and the value of the performance.[58]

These points are evident. Judge Ormond begins with his own opinion and at (relative) length. His own inclination, he says, speaking personally, almost informally, would be to find for the plaintiff. He moves through the facts that are relevant to his view and then briefly, formally, summarizes the conclusion that his brethren reached. But the last line brings us somehow back to his view of things. The decision in favor of the widow must be reversed, "pursuant to the agreement of the parties." What does this mean? They agreed at some point, perhaps to take an appeal. It might be that it is pursuant to their previous agreement to take an appeal and submit to that

---

55 See Karl Llewellyn, (1981[1933]), *The Bramblebush*: *On Our Law and Its Study*, p. 38 on found facts and true facts, noting that it would be almost a miracle if these were the same. 'See on the actual historical context of the *Kirksey* litigation Wiliiam Casto and Val Ricks 2006), 'Dear Sister Antillico: The Story of Kirksey v. Kirksey', 94 *Georgetown Law Journal* 321. pp. 321-397.

56 F. Pollack (1906), *Principles of Contract at Law and in Equity*. (eds Gustave Wald and Samuel Williston). (New York: Baker Voorhis), p. 24.

57 Farnsworth records the use of *Kirksey* by Williston and others. See E. Allan Farnsworth (1987), "Casebooks: Contracts Scholarship in the Age of the Anthology", *Michigan Law Review* 85, 1406–62.

58 Arthur Corbin (1947), *Cases in the Law of Contracts*, 3rd edition. (St Paul, MN: West Publishing), pp. 382–3.

decision? But does that require a special statement? The language may even hint at something else perhaps that the parties could still agree, could still reconcile. After judgment, they could still resume family relations. But this is, doubtless, to read too much into the language.[59]

Kirksey v. Kirksey became part of the canon. It is reproduced in a number of casebooks to this day, and is cited in law reviews.[60] The rule is that Sister Antillico's reliance does not count. Thus, Williston said, summarizing the case that "The widow came as requested but it was held that no contract was created thereby." But Ormond thought that a contract was created by the widow's reliance. And he recorded his view. One point here is that the case is not about whether a brother-in-law must take care of his brother's widow. It was litigated in terms of contract, not a family obligation. Anyone could have made such a promise. If a court found consideration, it would be enforced.

The Changing Shape of the Family

The sense of obligation that motivated brother Kirksey to help the widow of his brother is not much discussed today. Our focus, when we talk about security, is the nuclear family. But here too the changes are noteworthy. Marriage and the definition and purposes of marriage are contested by issues of same-sex marriage. Moreover, the differences between marriage and non-marriage are not what they were. It is standard in work on the American family to say, in effect, that this is the worst of all times and that the challenges to the family structure that we face are new in human history. Thus, a recent book on the family begins: "In America, over the last thirty years, we've done something unprecedented. We've managed to transform marriage, the most basic and universal of human institutions, into something contested."[61]

If contested means "widely contested," it is conceivable that this is true. But more literally, it seems false. The history of feminist radical and utopian thought has almost always contested the idea of marriage. It has been noted that "If any particular language be studied, it is seen that the words of which it is composed change rather slowly in the course of ages, while the images these words evoke or the meaning attached to them changes ceaselessly."[62] It is striking, for example, that some writers who cite proof-texts from the Bible use ideas of family and the state as though these

59 In a case decided some years later, another version of a family case, the Alabama Court discussed *Kirksey* (referring to it as *Kirksey v. Jones* (see Casto and Ricks)) saying that the present case, involving a father's promise to make a gift of a plantation and slaves to his sons, was not as strong as *Kirksey*. The later case involved a request for specific performance, which Sister Antillico was not seeking. John Ormond was on the panel.

60 See Allan Farnsworth, "Contracts Scholarship in the Age of the Anthology", *Michigan Law Review* 85, 1406–62.

61 Linda Waite and Maggie Gallagher, (2000), *The Case for Marriage*, p.1.

62 Gustav Le Bon (2002), *The Crowd: A Study of the Popular Mind* (reprint) (New York: Dover), p. 62.

were constant over millennia.[63] This, of course, is another reason for the idea that everyone liked marriage. Those alive in the last 30 years cannot be right. Marriage has changed so many times, in so many places, that it must be that someone wanted these changes. Which means that the institution has always been contested.

But the point here is not to attack or defend to marriage. Rather, it is to argue that the linkage between marriage–family–security has broken down, and that it is therefore necessary to rethink the ways in which we, collectively, think about security. This section does not present the case for marriage, in the hope that we will return somehow to some earlier world.[64] The concern here is with images, and particularly the images of marriage and the family that underlie government policy.

The idea that the family and the state stand in a significant relation to each other, that the family is a little commonwealth, that the health of the state requires healthy families, that the family is the foundation of the state, all of these are commonplace ideas in the West.[65]

But there is a problem here. The proposition that the state somehow is built on the family is not entirely obvious to generations that understand marriage largely in terms of private choices of individuals to facilitate their own happiness. How can the fate of the nation depend on such a fragile and unpredictable thing as the love between two people? This question—which describes a form of marriage that is not of course universal—is intensified by the realization that certain functions of the family—the education of children, for example—largely (though not entirely) have been taken over by the modern state. Again, we wonder how the family built on marriage can be seen as so publicly important.

Yet we know that it is seen as important. We see, for example, that politicians call for a return to marriage, a reinstatement of traditional family values. They believe that the family is in serious and social ways important. Sometimes this is argued in terms of training for citizenship.[66] But here, the argument has to do with security for individuals. Even if the state is supposed to protect individuals in the same way that the authorities were once supposed to save his people from dearth,[67] the state in calculating its responsibility, assumes the presence of the family.

But it seems possible that the family that it assumes is not the family we have. To that extent, the state will misconceive its role. In thinking about the New Deal,

---

63 See Mark Noll, (1995) *Scandal of the Evangelical Mind* (Grand Rapids, MI: William B. Eerdmans).

64 Which as Carl Schneider has noted, did not exist in any case. See Carl Schneider (1985), "Moral Discourse and the Transformation of American Family Law", *Michigan Law Review* 83, 1803–79. See also Carl E. Schneider (1992), "The Channelling Function in Family Law", *Hofstra Law Review* 20, 495–532.

65 See Lee Teitelbaum (1985), "Family History and Family Law", *Wisconsin Law Review* 1185, 1135–82.

66 Anne Dailey (1993), "Constitutional Privacy and The Just Family", *Tulane Law Journal* 67, 955–1032.

67 See John Walter and Keith Wrightson (1976), "Dearth and the Social Order in Early Modern England", *Past and Present* 71, May, 22–42.

"welfare planners and legislators might especially have paused to consider whether traditional legal concepts of property, residence, income, the makeup of the family and the responsibilities of family members" were relevant, TenBrock wrote.[68] These were ideas originating in other contexts and properly governing other relationships he said. It might be urged that other ideas were more appropriate for welfare programs. "If one confines himself to the planning area of the federal Social Security Act, and again narrows that to the public assistance provisions of that measure, it is clear that no such act of imaginative originality took place."[69]

To the extent that the modern family is built on romantic love, it has always had in it an immense contradiction. That very love that is seen on the one hand to be endless, eternal, larger than anything else in the world, is also on the basis of common experience, to be finite. Of the many kinds of love, the romantic love on which we in America found the family is the one most likely to change its substance in the course of time. The point is elaborated by C.S. Lewis: "The grim joke is that this Eros whose voice seems to speak from the eternal realm is not himself necessarily even permanent. He is notoriously the most mortal of our loves. The world rings with complaints of his fickleness. What is baffling is the combination of this fickleness with his protestations of permanency."

Yet, Lewis continues, "Eros is in a sense right to make this promise. The event of falling in love is of such a nature that we are right to reject as intolerable the idea that it should be transitory." But then we see the difficulty. "Can we be in this selfless liberation for a lifetime? Hardly for a week. Between the best possible lovers this high condition is intermittent." What then will be the impact of this in marriage? These lapses, Lewis thinks, "will not destroy a marriage between two "decent and sensible" people. The couple whose marriage will certainly be endangered by them, and possibly ruined, are those who have idolised Eros."[70] It may be that this is as good a description of the modern situation as any other.

The focus here is on the family. If marriage and the family rest on the state, it is also the case that the state has been seen to rest on the marriage and on the family. The links are as clear today in the United States as ever.[71] Quite recently, for example, we have seen a call for the support and encouragement of marriage as a remedy for social problems with reference to people receiving welfare.[72] The proposal is sometimes linked to arguments that the great society, by providing incentives for benefits outside of marriage, in fact injured marriage and the family and that we ought to somehow turn the clock back.

---

68 Jacobus TenBrock (1954), "The Impact of Welfare Law Upon Family Law", *California Law Review* 42, 458–85, p. 459.

69 Ibid. at p. 458. See also Bruce Ackerman and Anne Alstott *The Stakeholder Society* (New Haven, CT: Yale University Press).

70 C.S. Lewis, (1963) *The Four Loves* (London: Fontana).

71 In other countries this may be more or less true.

72 Matthew Cooper, "Going to the Chapel", *TIME*, June 10, 2002, p. 31.

But going back to the 1960s presents problems. Not least is that marriage and the family do not look the same today in the United States as they did in 1960. This is true generally and across the population. No-fault divorce and a high tolerance of divorce, plus a high tolerance of premarital cohabitation presumably are related to the change.

We can contrast the extended family with "blended family". The extended family was fixed, and defined, built on marriage, and served many obvious economic functions including employer of last resort. Blended family may be rich emotionally, and reflect existing configurations and loyalty, existing in the moment but like certain forms of modern art it is almost defined as fleeting. Putting it strongly, we could say that the blended family is those people who happen to be around at the moment.

The attempt to create stability in this situation has led to an interest in the use of contract law both before marriage and as part of a readjustment of ongoing marriages. The arguments against the use of contracts have been elaborated as extensively as the arguments for contracts, but not enough attention has been given to the problem of remedies. It is not merely the problem of the mindset of the parties, issues of interpretation, and whether individualized contract will preserve the values we wish to present when these are social or collective. The further question is what law can do to enforce these contracts. Here, the experience with some ancient uses of marriage contracts may have something to say.

Marriage Contracts: Illustrations from Islamic Law

As a general point, contract is a useful device for particularizing many kinds of arrangements. While the Western marriage contract is often seen as an adhesion contract, it is, first, useful to see it as a contract and, second, useful to see what kinds of variations the law of contract might facilitate. These issues can be seen clearly in the case of the Islamic marriage contract, which assumes negotiated marriage contracts as part of the basic family structure. The advantage of a focus on the Islamic contract is that we can see the use of a marriage contract in a setting in which it is viewed as legitimate and appropriate. It is not necessary to debate whether it commercializes or commodifies human relationships or reduces soft, altruistic motivations to hard self-interested exchanges.

Sir Norman Anderson observed some 30 years ago that Islamic Family Law was "almost the only part of Islamic law which is still applied by courts all over the world to the vast majority of Muslims."[73] Some of this is true because some countries continue to use religious legal systems as personal law. It is also true in countries that do not incorporate religious legal systems because individuals choose to use religious law. "Contract" may enter the story in two ways. Some traditions offer contractual solutions at least for some problems. Thus, some states that use Islamic

---

73 Norman Anderson (1969), "Islamic Family Law", in Mary Ann Glendon (ed.) *International Encyclopaedia of Comparative Law Vol. IV: Persons and Family.* (Tübingen and Mouton, The Hague: J.C.B. Mohr (Paul Siebeck)), pp. 11–105.

family law have recognized the possible use of such contracts within Islamic law. In those states that do not, contracts born in religious law may come into litigation through general contract ideas.

That the Islamic marriage contract is conceptually contractual (rather than having an emphasis on status or covenant) is clear in this description from a Pakistani judge: "The rights arising out of an Islamic marriage contract are not the gifts of any legislative body of a country. They emanate from the proposal and the acceptance of the parties made at marriage time." The contract is understood as simultaneously temporal and religious.[74] The religious marriage contract, when described in these terms, suggests that the conversation on the commercialization of marriage through contract, a conversation common in the United States, makes no sense against a particular background. Similarly, the idea that there is little room for variations in the marriage contract is more culturally specific than we (Americans) ordinarily see. The 1956 United Nations (UN) report on the status of women began with a discussion of variations, and then noted that this was not a possibility in legal regimes derived from the English common law.[75]

In any case, there is considerable interest among Islamic women in the idea of using the contractual aspects of Islamic marriage to protect women's rights, for example to stipulate that women may work without a husband's permission, and may divorce him (using his right to divorce as delegated to her).

Thus, we have a description of the efforts to draft a model Islamic Marriage Contract:

> As for a specific example of where Islamic law is a mechanism for empowerment of women, we have been working on: creating a model Islamic marriage contract. In Islamic law, marriage is primarily a contract, not a sacrament, and there are quite a lot of specific elements that can go into that contract. Both parties have the opportunity to include all of their particulars in that relationship via this contract ...
>
> Yet, on many issues affecting marriage, there are differences of opinion within Islamic jurisprudence, and you can choose which particular opinion will apply to you in your marriage. So, for example, people include clauses against polygamy, equalizing divorce rights of both parties, even regarding custody; all these kinds of issues can be worked out in advance.[76]

---

74 Tanzil ur Rahman quoted in David Pearl and Werner Menski (1998), *Muslim Family Law*, 3rd edition. (London: Sweet and Maxwell), p. 176.

75 "Legal Status of Married Women" (1958) Commission on the Status of Women United Nations, New York (reports submitted by the secretary general): "The laws of many countries not only prescribe the "statutory regime" but also set forth in detail, alternative "contractual regimes" (*régimes conventionnels*) which the prospective spouses may adopt as a whole in a pre-nuptial agreement ..."

76 *Fordham Urban Law Journal* (1997), "Remarks: Panel Discussion: Models of Successful 'Religion and Lawyering' Programs", *Fordham Urban Law Journal* 917, p. 933, comments of Asifa Quaraisha (panel discussion on models of successful religion and lawyering programs).

Today, we see some other issues. Religious law can be used as illustrative of contract terms to suggest the sort of substantive regulation we might be thinking about.

Initially, however, there is a question of contractual intent. Are these verbal acts ceremonial only or do the parties understand them as contracts having substantively binding aspects under state law? This issue becomes important as a background to this discussion since if religious contracts are not really contracts, they can provide no particular enforceable solutions to the issues—particularly relating to gender equality—which are of concern.

As to the problem of variation by agreement, one question is historical: under what circumstances did religious legal systems (or legal systems in general) accept the possibility of variation by agreement and what kind of provisions were accepted?[77] Certain statutes acknowledge the possibility of stipulations in a fairly detailed way.[78] One question, then, is whether at some moment, a religious legal system is prepared to use the possibility of variation by agreement as a way of solving a particular problem. Here, one thinks of the discussions of the problem of the *get* (Jewish divorce) and the possibility of solving some part of that problem by a provision in the *ketubah*, the Jewish marriage contract, a solution to which some parts of the community are more receptive than other parts. Here, too, one finds discussion of ameliorating clauses in the Islamic marriage contract. If included in the contract, and if either complied with or enforced, at least in theory, individual variations are, it seems, possible.[79]

But, of course, contract as an idea raises its own problems. If some clauses are good for women, others might be not so desirable. They might involve waiver of rights rather than expansion of rights.[80]

In ordinary secular contracts, the solution to a problem is often a legally mandated term, a legally mandated warranty, for example. But that warranty can be disclaimed unless we say, by one device or another, legislative or judicial, that it cannot be. At that point, we have a standard form contract.

But is this subject to the idea of a religious, judicial or legislative conscientious objection? That is, if we, as the state, mandated compulsory divorce insurance in a

---

77 See Lucy Carroll (1982), "Stipulations in Muslim Marriage Contract Important means of protecting the Position of the South Asian Muslim Wife", *Modern Asian Studies* 16, 277–309 ; also Lynn Welchman's research on the West Bank, cited in Pearl and Menski *Muslim Family Law*, p. 178; also Nelly Henna (1996), "Marriage Among Merchant Families in 17th Century Cairo", in Amira Sonbol (ed.) *Women, the Family and Divorce Laws in Islamic History*, p.147.

78 See particularly Kuwait.

79 Some Islamic personal status laws refer to them.

80 A husband might insist on stipulations that maintained his control over, for example, his wife's employment.

certain amount, could Islamic couples—the wife in the Shah Bano case when she was young—have received a religious exemption?[81]

Then there is the issue of custom. It has been noted that:

> While rights for Muslim women have been affirmed social customs continue to dominate, still making them unavailable. Such customs include arranged marriages in which the consent of the women (and sometimes of the man) involved is not sought; the appropriation of the dowry by the father as a compensation for the loss of his daughter, even though Islamic law guarantees it to the bride alone; the lack of equal treatment of wives in polygamous marriages; and the abuse of the privilege of divorce (especially in the Gulf region) in which the husband simply states 'you are divorced' three times, without recourse to arbitration or attempt at reconciliation.[82]

Are these customs part of the contract even though not required by religious law? Are they enforceable? Can they be negated? How? (They might be, assumed as terms, under modern American approaches to the interpretation of commercial contracts.) Are they easier to negate through statute (because individual intent would not matter), or harder? (Because as a political matter they might more accurately reflect the community interests.)

Other difficult issues relate to the idea of enforcement. Clearly, enforcement does not necessarily mean specific performance for example, and contractual options—following the UCC—might include agreed-upon remedies, as well as statutory remedies.[83] It is also clear that remedies are a cultural institution, and that in the American culture, for example, certain remedies are assumed to be inappropriate. We do not hang people for violating the sanctity of contract. Our sense of the appropriate remedy for breach of contracts starts, conventionally, with money damages. When our thinking moves to what the law of contracts considers the atypical remedy, some sort of specific performance, we run into serious difficulty in the domestic context.

To begin with, it is clear that in many family cases, money is not an adequate remedy and our thinking does have to turn to other possibilities. Thus, surrogacy contracts (in which one wants the child), promises to give a get (a Jewish religious

---

81 Shah Bano was a women divorced after a 44-year marriage. Her husband maintained that he was not obliged to provide maintenance under the standards of the secular law but was only bound by religious law. The controversy in India over support/maintenance orders under Islamic law and the law of India continued for some years. See P. Jagonmohan Reddy (1987), "Shah Bano Verdict and Muslim Law", in Asghar Ali Engineer (ed.) *The Shah Bano Controversy* (Hyderabad: Orient Longman), pp. 41–45; Anika Rahman (1990), Note, "Religious Rights Versus Women's Rights in India: A Test Case for International Human Rights Law", *Columbia Journal of Transnational law* 28, 473–82. Vrinde Nerain (1998), "Women's Rights and the Accommodation of Difference", *Southern California Review of Law and Women's Studies* 8, 37.

82 Yvonne Haddad (1998), "Islam and Gender: Dilemmas in the Changing Arab World", in Y. Haddad and J. Esposito (eds) *Islam, Gender and Social Change*, p. 7.

83 These paragraphs draw in part on Weisbrod (1994), "The Way We Live Now", *Utah Law Review* 777–816.

divorce), and promises for the religious upbringing of children all present instances in which money is not really the desired remedy. Yet other more direct remedies may be barred, because, for example, personal services contracts are not specifically enforceable and the Constitution guarantees "the free exercise of religion," with all the complexities of that idea.

Whether these agreements in fact should be directly enforced will depend, as it has always, on a policy judgment itself heavily influenced by underlying social factors, including the behavior, intentions and reliance of the individuals involved, and the judicial reading of those factors.

Of course any contract may still be "unconscionable" or "unfair," and thus unenforceable.[84] The problem for us is not so much judicial power to police domestic contracts for fairness and the like as our judicial standard, which will vary greatly depending on the kind of state, the kind of social issue, they are considering. What are the objectives of the state in these contexts? What is fair? How do we know it? Where do we look for state policy on the question?

It has recently been emphasized that, even in the West, the idea that multiple forms of religion can exist in a single state is acceptable is relatively new. Professor Thomas Franck makes the point by comparing the language of Chancellor Kent in the blasphemy case *People v. Ruggles* to something that an Islamic fundamentalist might say today. The Ayotollah Khomenei could not have put it better, Franck writes.[85]

The issues of ceremonials and contracts being recognized at all is a question for systems that link church and state fairly closely, either by being structurally theocratic or by considering themselves more loosely as operating with in a religious tradition. "A Christian Nation." "An Islamic State." The whole emphasis on the rights of individuals may be secondary both to the larger state and to the minority religion asking for recognition.

---

84 See Uniform Commercial Code § 2–302. Even aside from such a direct policing doctrine, results can be achieved by manipulation of technical doctrines, although "[c]overt tools are never reliable tools." Karl N. Llewellyn (1939), Book Review, *Harvard Law Review* 52, 700–21, p. 703.

85 Thomas Franck, "Is Personal Freedom a Western Value?" *American Journal of International Law* 91, 593–603.

The liberal secular state stresses the rights of the individual as a foundational point.[86] In the system of liberal thought, individuals are thought to have free choice of religions, including the right to choose religious courts[87] or to change religions.[88]

Domestic courts dealing with religious marriage contracts can refuse to enforce them in a variety of theories. In the United States, they might say that judicial enforcement of such a contract violated the establishment clause.[89] A Canadian court found that the religious contract providing for a return of the mahr (payment by the husband to the wife) was unenforceable, in a system without an establishment clause, because religious obligations, like the Christian contractual obligation to love, are non-judiciable in state courts.[90] (The court used US Supreme Court material on "religious thickets" or entanglement.) Or, a contract may be unenforceable because at least one of the parties lacked contractual capacity.[91]

The questions become whether individual choices are too damaging to the individuals themselves to be permitted—(even though free)—and whether we

86 1975 was the international year of the women. In 1973, six countries denied suffrage to women.

87 "The norm of prohibition of discrimination against women would not be implicated where women themselves select religious tribunals as the forum for adjudication, and where women have full access to secular courts. But where religious tribunals assert the power to adjudicate the legal rights of women or where national legislation embodies religious law, the status of the rights guaranteed by the Discrimination Against Women Convention may be implicated." Theodor Meron (1986), *Human Rights Law Making in the United Nations*, Oxford, Clarendon Press p. 156.

88 While the Universal Declaration of Human Rights (Article 18) protects the right to change religion, later documents are less clear on the issue. See generally Mark Janis and Carolyn Evans (eds) (1999), *Religion and International Law*, 2nd edition. (Martinus Nijhoff, The Hague), pp. 385-400.

89 *Avitzur v. Avitzur*, 446 NE2d 136 (1983) (upholding enforcement of ketuba); *Aziz v. Aziz*, 488 NYS2d 123 (1985) (upholding enforcement of mahr).

90 *Sam Kaddoura v. Hammoud*, C J lexis 2504 (1998); The husband and wife are described as "attractive, engaging and strong minded young people", who identified with the religious community but were not orthodox. The wife sought both the deferred mahr and exemplary damages. Both were denied. There is no discussion of American cases involving similar contracts. Note also the description of the husband who seemed to the judge somewhat "offensive and dishonorable" in knowingly participating in traditional practices, including the promise of the $30,000 in the deferred mahr which he then refused to pay when these "customs and practices worked to his financial detriment." Rutherford, J. opinion as to Costs, 1999 Ont. C.J. Lexis173, p. 2.

91 A marriage contract between those who are under age will raise this issue. And over-age? We see this as a capacity issue, or perhaps one involving undue influence or even duress. A rule of pre-revolutionary Russia said that those over 80 could not marry because they could not procreate. See Harold Berman (1963[1950]) *Justice in the USSR: An interpretation of Soviet Law*, revised edition. (Cambridge, MA: Harvard University Press), p. 332. If 15 is the recommended standard for the age of marriage for the young, are we ready to set an age for the elderly?

should see someone's situation as so benighted[92] that they should not be permitted to choose.[93]

At the same time, it may be worth noting that there is a question whenever the consent of the victim is not required. This is particularly true when we say that the victim fails to perceive the possibility that the situation can or should be remedied. At this point, our analysis of the problem must take into account the issue not only of ignorance or degradation but also of disagreement, or lack of consensus on the desirability of the particular goal.

If one considers the question of human rights and marriage, one of the points that initially suggests itself is that the precise trouble spots that might be identified as implicating human rights have varied over time. Thus, in seventeenth century England, one issue was whether Quakers and Jews could use their own contracts.[94] The question could then be discussed not so much in terms of contracts, as ceremonies. Where a particular religious ceremony is the norm, what does the system do with those adhering to a minority religion? This remained an issue for some time. It was still a significant point in the Krishnasawmi report of 1959.[95]

Today, we see some issue about the availability of civil marriages in some countries, some question of what status religious marriage contracts have within a system of secular state regulated marriage.[96]

The traditional legal approach to marriage in the nineteenth century was similar enough to slavery to be uncomfortable. And the emphasis on equality in the Convention against Discrimination against Women[97] makes plain that in fact equality is dramatically lacking in many places at this time. And if monogamy is not the "marriage" in question, inequality is clear, both in the fact that only the men have multiple partners as well as the fact that polygamy as practised may be very close to slavery.[98]

---

92 Though not legally incompetent.

93 Or even if formally allowed to choose, may not have money or education sufficient to choose or complain if denied rights.

94 See Bromley, pp. 37–8.

95 Arcot Krishnaswami (1960), "Study of Discrimination in the Matter of Religious Rights and Practices", UN Doc. E/CN.4/Sub.2/200/Rev.1 United Nations Publication Catalogue No. 60.XIV.2, pp. 36, 37.

96 Leo Pfeffer (1953), *Church, State and Freedom* (Boston, MA: Beacon). Marriage then was a civil contract, though it might involve a variety of religious functionaries.

97 See Article 16 of the 1979 Convention, forbidding discrimination against women, referring to equality between men and women.

98 Polygamy is an example of voluntary slavery in some philosophical discussions. See Joel Feinberg, discussing J.S. Mill, J. Feinberg (1983), "Autonomy, Sovereignty and Privacy", *Notre Dame Law Review* 58, 445–92. We would today stress questions of post-divorce property rights (an issue in the Western world and in India) and questions on inequality in access to divorce. But perhaps it is more like drudgery (a distinction offered by John Locke (2004), *Two Treatises of Government* (ed. Peter Laslett) (Cambridge: Cambridge University Press), second treatise, p. 285.

Free consent to marriage means both free choice of the status and the individual. Issues of the proper minimum age for marriage—both largely in the present world issues involving women, though they also can and do involve men, are in fact essentially about contractual capacity.[99]

Probably the rules and institutions themselves must be understood in a cultural context. An approach to maintenance that assumes that a divorced woman will be supported by her relatives will not look the same in a traditional world of extended family structures and in a modern world in which relatives communicate with each other by e-mail across oceans and continents.[100] Polygamy looks different in Africa and in Paris.[101] It may be, as Clifford Geertz suggested, that the assumption that one rule will cover all cases is not universal but provincial.[102]

Perhaps for us, as much as for earlier generations, marriage is a problem as much as a solution. We can sympathize with Emerson's comment, derived perhaps from an earlier source, that marriage is an open question as is clear from the fact that those on the outside want to get in while those were inside want to get out.[103] The question becomes particularly complicated when we admit cultural variation to our ideas of marriage.

The first part of this discussion raised the question, what do the international instruments mean by marriage and divorce?, and opened a range of possible meanings that are available once one leaves particular cultural settings. The second part reviewed issues of contract law that might arise within a specific cultural setting dealing with issues of contracts and contractual variation of a particular form of marriage.

The general point is that the family is so basic and pervasive that it is often simply taken as background, not even included in the account of institutions for assistance.[104]

---

99 Child marriage sometimes involves males. Margaret Cole notes a Chinese tradition under which diseased children were married rather than have them die celibate. Margaret Cole (1938), *Marriage* (London: Dent), p. 48 citing J.H. Gray (1878), *China.*

100 Shoba Sarayan (1999), "A far flung clan gathers on-line to put Aunt Sheila to Rest", *New York Times* August 19, p. G7, describing Hindu family meeting on-line from all over India and all over the world.

101 On polygamy in the United States, see Irwin Altman (1996), "Polygamous Family Life: The Case of Contemporary Mormon Fundamentalists", *Utah Law Review* 2, 367–92. On polygamy among African immigrants living in the suburbs of Paris, see Marlise Simons (1996), "African Women in France Battling Polygamy", *New York Times*, January 26, pp. A1–2.

102 See Clifford Geertz (1984), "Anti Anti Relativism", *American Anthropological Association* 83.

103 Ralph Waldo Emerson (1990[1850]), "Montaigne or Skeptic", in Robert D. Richardson (ed.) *Selected Essays Lectures and Poems*, pp. 281–5.

104 Jacob Hacker, as noted above, sees the importance of private institutions, and particularly private health insurance and private pensions, as institutions through which in the modern world, individuals are provided with security. His treatment focuses on private

The art critic Robert Hughes describes Norman Rockwell's 1943 painting Freedom from Want (one of the series referring to Franklin Roosevelt's Four Freedoms) first in terms of family: "The great social fact was family continuity, generation on generation. It was a world unmarked by doubt, violence or greed." And as to the mountainous turkey in that picture, he describes it as an "image of virtuous abundance".[105]

The present book considers the importance of private and public (defining private more broadly) but notes that there is a sense in which in the modern world, in which the state is engaged in so much activity that touches all aspects of life, it is possible to say that there is a sense in which the public touches if not absolutely everything, at least a vast amount. The constitutional doctrine of state action is one attempt to draw a line between public and private activity, between things governed by the constitution and things free of the constitution, but as is sometimes noted, it is a somewhat difficult question. Even as to the family, usually considered "private", it seems obvious, from a legal realist perspective, that the law (government) defines what is and isn't a family and sets rules and then creates expectations about what families should and should not do. Insurance also, though "private" in the sense of non-government, is regulated by law and rests on the foundational legal institution of the law of contracts.

The forms that family support take are highly various. Some are largely emotional, some are directly material, some involving paying fees to third parties. The family can be seen as an insuring institution, but is has inadequacies here. And it has ambiguities. A well-known book on retirement strategies includes a discussion of smaller as against bigger houses. The book suggests that if people buy a smaller house, there will still, very likely, be room for children and grandchildren who visit. If not, they can stay at hotels. And after all, "you can't be expected to maintain a big expensive house just so that relatives will have a place to stay a few days a year."[106] Among the questions here are some involving self image—do the owners of the big house imagine themselves as always available as a refuge for many people?—and some involving the meaning of language. The word "relatives" includes children. But are relatives and children connections of the same weight or intensity?

Is there a failure-of-imagination problem here as deep as that sometimes discussed with reference to rich and poor? Do those without children have only theoretical understandings of claims, based on blood, history, life patterns, which are real to parents? Does this make possible an undifferentiated use of language which would be more difficult for those with more context? Are there other instances in

---

and public institutions, where the private are non-governmental institutions and the public are governmental institutions. The family is perceived as involving unmediated voluntary transfers.

105 Robert Hughes (1992) "Norman Rockwell" in *Nothing if Not Critical*, Part 5, *Americans* (New York: Penguin), pp. 230–33, p. 232. (For more on the Norman Rockwell turkey, see Chapter 4 of the present volume.)

106 Fred Brock (2004), *Retire on Less Than You Think*. (New York: Time Books, Henry Holt), p. 57.

which the same issue may manifest itself? For example: Is a "single" man, a newly divorced spouse with children and grandchildren, in the same position in terms of responsibility and obligation, as a single man who has never married or had children at all? Clearly we don't think so. And we don't think that "single mother" is a term that can, for purposes of policy, cover all cases, and tend to distinguish between the never married and the divorced, for example.

The debate over "marriage" and "divorce" can resolve some questions here, but there are other possibilities. Conventional private insurance, for example, has a role here. Insurance is an aspect of family support, as is plain from the following observation of Justice Hugo Black: "Perhaps no modern commercial enterprise directly affects so many persons in all walks of life as does the insurance business. Insurance touches the home, the family and the occupation or the business of almost every person in the United States."[107] And as Tom Baker has noted, whether or not a company is willing to insure a wage earner will greatly affect the lives of the children of the family.[108] The next chapter deals with insurance and its strengths and weaknesses in relation to security.

---

107 *United States v. South Eastern Underwriters Association*, 322 US 533 (1944), p. 540.

108 Tom Baker (2002–03), "Containing the Promise of Insurance: Adverse Selection and Risk Classification", *Connecticut Insurance Law Journal* 9, 371–96.

Chapter 3

Security through Insurance

> Insurance ... presents a mechanism through which an organized group comes to the assistance of an individual, without those negative effects which follow in the suit of gratuitous relief. Insurance has the moral advantage of a contractual obligation. It has proven its efficiency to compensate for losses due to extraneous forces in many fields. Insurance, therefore, is preferable to charity.
>
> I.M. Rubinow[1]

If the extremes of public and private can be represented by government support of security and the private activities of the family, we commonly see the activities of groups like insurance companies as occupying a middle ground.[2] The companies are "private" in the sense that they are non-governmental and are often market driven. They have, however, a clear public dimension in that in America the industry as a whole is heavily regulated. As Jacob Hacker has argued, this "private" activity of insurance companies should be understood as central to the American provision of security against various risks. Moreover, in a way parallel to the discussion of the family in Chapter 2 above, insurance is built on contract, so that its protections can be, at least in theory, highly individual, and, to the extent that contract means "legal" contract, we again see the hand of the state.

While there are some who had doubts about insurance (described below), insurance companies and their customers came to believe that insurance was the way in which love of family was expressed and that all husbands ought to carry adequate insurance on their own lives. Of course the target families were the middle-class families that are, in general, the target families of the insurance industry. It is the middle-class family that has wage earners whose lives are taken to be of calculable economic value and who accumulate property that also requires insurance against fire and theft. Ericson, Doyle and Barry describe this family in Canada in terms of a particular kind of car: "The minivan is the icon of the Canadian nuclear family,

---

1 I.M. Rubinow (1913), *Social Insurance* (New York: Henry Holt), p. 421.

2 Chapter Three draws heavily on Weisbrod (1999–2000), "Insurance and the Utopian Idea", *Connecticut Insurance Law Journal* 6, 383–422, and on Weisbrod (2003–04), "War, Insurance and Some Problems of Community", *Connecticut Insurance Law Journal* 10, 103–11, p. 104.

symbolizing good values, stability, conservatism and preferred insurance risk."[3] That family will also be responsible about risk reduction, careful about fire prevention and driver education, scrupulous about record keeping.[4]

As Deborah Stone has noted, the insurance industry has at its center ambivalence in relation to the family that involves a class differentiation. Quoting David Moss, she notes that the goal of insurance is to provide security to those who have something to lose, and not to protect those who have nothing to lose.[5] The industry encourages ideas of mutual support and leaning on others through insurance in relation to the wealthy, while describing the same behavior on the part of the poor as an unworthy dependency.[6]

We tend to assume a world with insurance.[7] The absence of insurance is usually understood either in terms of financial restriction or conscientious objection. For most middle-class people, the desirability of insurance, and its general availability in the absence of special problems, is assumed. But perhaps a more general examination of the theory and practice of insurance would be useful.

We have, in the world of imagination and literary reference, another idea. It is precisely a world without insurance that is associated in the Western tradition with the story of catastrophic and inexplicable affliction represented by Job. It is useful initially to look at the story of Job to outline some of the arguments about insurance that are concealed by our widespread acceptance of the institution. The chapter then goes on to consider benefits of insurance in terms of community, and, then the down side of community, problems of exclusion, which in this context means inability to buy insurance, either because the buyer or the risk is excluded.

Job: A World without Insurance

The story of Job is part of the Hebrew Bible. It is given this way:

---

3 Richard Ericson, Aaron Doyle and Dean Barry (2003), *Insurance as Governance*. (Toronto: University of Toronto Press), p. 283.

4 Ibid.

5 Deborah Stone, "Beyond Moral Hazard: Insurance as Moral Opportunity", in Tom Baker and Jonathan Simon (2002), *Embracing Risk: The Changing Culture of Insurance and Responsibility* (Chicago: University of Chicago Press), p. 59.

6 Martha McClusky "Rhetoric of Risk and the Redistribution of Social Insurance", in Baker and Simon, *Embracing Risk*, pp. 146–70. We are today, in the United States, witnessing a wrinkle in this basic dichotomy as we see a middle-class population soon-to-be-aged attempting to create eligibility for Medicaid, a program designed for the poor, by what is in effect a variation of the kind of estate planning long favored by the wealthy as a way to limit taxes. The once middle-class recipient of Medicaid becomes someone who is voluntarily poor—or "quasi-poor" or "artificially poor", in order either to preserve assets for a healthy spouse attempting to live as the couple had lived, or to leave an estate for children and grandchildren. See discussion in Lee Teitelbaum (1992), "Intergenerational Responsibility and Family Obligations", *Utah Law Review*, 765–802.

7 See generally Tom Baker (2003), *Insurance Law and Policy* (New York: Aspen).

> 1. There was a man in the land of Uz, whose name was Job; and that man was blameless and upright, one who feared God, and turned away from evil. 2. There were born to him seven sons and three daughters. 3. He had seven thousand sheep, three thousand camels, five hundred yoke of oxen, and five hundred she-asses, and very many servants; so that this man was the greatest of all the people of the east ...[8]

The story continues with a wager between God and Satan, in which Satan says:

> "Thou hast blessed the work of his hands, and his possessions have increased in the land. But put forth thy hand now, and touch all that he has, and he will curse thee to thy face."[9]

> And the LORD said to Satan, "Behold, all that he has is in your power; only upon himself do not put forth your hand."[10]

Satan causes Job to lose everything he has: camels, servants, children.

The book of Job concerns itself with the problem of Job's suffering, and its lack of justification. Of interest here is not the major part of the text, but only the epilogue, the so-called happy ending.[11]

> And the LORD restored the fortunes of Job, when he had prayed for his friends; and the LORD gave Job twice as much as he had before ... And the LORD blessed the latter days of Job more than his beginning; and he had fourteen thousand sheep, six thousand camels, a thousand yoke of oxen, and a thousand she-asses. He had also seven sons and three daughters ...[12]

The restoration given to Job is provided by the same God who originally permitted/caused Job's suffering. But, what if it had been provided by an insurance company? What if the first question for Job was not "Why Me?" or "Why should the Righteous Suffer?" but "Am I insured for This?" Of course, if Job had been insured, the afflictions could have included the insolvency of the Insurer.[13] But the idea that Job might have insured his wealth, or the lives of his children seems to change the story.

---

8 Job 1:1–10, Herbert May and Bruce Metzger (eds) (1962), *Oxford Annotated Bible* (revised standard). (New York: Oxford University Press).

9 Ibid., Job 1:11.

10 Ibid., Job 1:12.

11 See Martin Copenhaven (1994), "Risking a Happy Ending", in *Christian Century*, v. III, p. 923. "It is not difficult to see why many commentators have concluded that the epilogue comes from a different source and was simply tacked on. After the bold cadences of the poetry that has gone before, the epilogue is told in prose—and it seems, well, prosaic. It is the happily-ever-after ending of a fairy tale."

12 May and Metzger, *Oxford Annotated Bible*, Job 42:10 ff.

13 See Terence O'Donnell (1936), *History of Life Insurance: In its Formative Years*. (Chicago: America Conservation), pp. 751–2 (quoting William Penn who after an unsatisfactory experience wrote "Ensurers fail much.")

To the extent that it mitigates, insurance influences the meaning of human suffering in relation to certain events.[14] It is in that sense, like all other social reforms, which, when successful, have the effect of leaving us with the question of love and death in ideal conditions.

The story of Job concludes on a note of restoration, if not quite of the status *quo ante*, at least something quite close. Job has more money, no children, but the expectation of future children, presumably by way of substitution. As a commentator on Job wrote, modern values as to children are quite different from the ancient ones.[15] That there should have been changes on this point is no surprise. Compare modern Western values with the tribal values described by Ruth Benedict as to tribes in which restitution—a new spouse for a murdered spouse—was considered an appropriate remedy.[16]

It seems possible that to the extent that insurance is restitutionary or restorative, it is aligned with a religious tradition that reaches the ultimate point in the idea of Messianic restoration. To the extent that it attempts to project future earnings (for example) insurance is more problematic.

The usual explanations hold that the hostility to life insurance has roots in concern with commodification of human life, that it reflects a lack of trust, a betting against God.[17] But, perhaps the idea of restitutionary remedies also has a role here. Certainly on this point we must first say something about the ending of Job, which involves more than restitution. Rushdoony reads Leviticus 5:14–16 as referring to "a case of sin where God was directly involved," in which case a fifth part was added to the restoration.[18] These are sins against God. But is this kind of statement a possible explanation for the double portion in Job?[19] Midrashic material contains a long description of Job's charity, including pledges to provide for widows and

14 If we compare the restoration of God with an insurance ending, we get several issues. First, the insurance company may or may not pay, according to its reading of the contract. Second, it will not pay more than the loss (let alone double the loss), and in some instances, the company may have subrogation rights under what is understood as an indemnity arrangement. Finally, it will pay because of the loss, not, for example, because Job has defended his friends.

15 See George Arthur Buttrick (ed.) (1951–57), *Interpreter's Bible*, Vol. III (New York: Abindgon-Cokesbury), p. 1196 (quoting A.S. Peake (1904) *The Century Bible*).

16 See Ruth Benedict (1989[1934]), *Patterns of Culture* (Boston, MA: Houghton Mifflin), p. 256.

17 See William T. Standen (1897), *The Ideal Protection*, p. 119.

18 John Rousas Rushdoony (1973), *Institutes of Biblical Law* (Phillipsburg, PA: Reformed Publishing), p. 276 (not discussing Job).

19 Is it, as Peake suggests through his citations, linked to a double portion for shame? (citing doubling in Isaiah 61:7 and Zachariah 9:12). See Peake cited in Buttrick, *Interpreter's Bible*, p. 345.

orphans if a sick husband should die.[20] The double portion, perhaps, balances an earlier account of generosity.

However, life insurance, as has been noted, is not really about restitution. It is not, as Jerry writes, focused on indemnification,[21] though it is sometimes described as having some component of indemnity.[22] Job does not receive lost profits.[23] It may be that here we have some sense of the answer to the question of why life insurance is different. It is not restitution, contrary to an assumption of economic theory, which considers an expectation interest as the equivalent of money in the bank. Further, life insurance, and the amount of insurance, is not—except at a psychological or rhetorical level—geared to a specific calculation about future support. It simply takes a number. Moreover, if life insurance is a projection of future support, it assumes that level of support through the individual life, which assumes employment future and thus limits the Divine Plan.[24]

If there are problems specific to life insurance, there may also be positive features. A positive value, unique to life insurance, was said to be altruism. It is a transaction in which the insured receives nothing, except of course, the knowledge that the family's future was secure.[25] This private altruism can be linked to a much larger community.

What is Insurance?

How should we think about the institution of insurance? It has for example a function not normally described as one of its functions and has a major impact—only winning the lottery would bring so much so quickly, and that is not built on death—on the

---

20 See Louis Ginzberg (1983), *Legends of the Jews* (Philadelphia, PA: Jewish Publication Society of America, pp. 230–31.

21 "Under the principle of indemnity, the insured's recovery should not exceed the loss. Life insurance, although it has some indemnity aspects (such as reimbursing the beneficiaries for the loss of income caused by the insured's death), is not indemnity insurance in the strictest sense. In most cases, no effort is made to place a value on the insured's life; an individual can purchase an unlimited amount of insurance on his or her own life." Robert Jerry II (1987), *Understanding Insurance Law* (New York, Lexis Nexis), p. 628; see also Spencer L. Kimball and Don A. Davis (1962), "The Extension of Insurance Subrogation", *Michigan Law Review* 60, 841–72.

22 See Standen, *The Ideal Protection*, p. 70.

23 Unless that idea explains the doubling, i.e. doubling makes up for lost profits.

24 The Divine Plan is limited in that the worker might lose his position in the labor market at any time. Note that the Divine Plan can be seen as extending over generations. See C.S. Lewis (1946), *That Hideous Strength* (New York: Macmillan), p. 278 (referring to contraception as an attack on the Divine Plan).

25 Compare viatical transactions. A viatical settlement is an "act by a person who is terminally ill of cashing in a life insurance policy to pay for the necessary associated illness, medical expenses and final wishes," Harvey W. Rubin (1995), *Barron's Dictionary of Insurance Terms*, 3rd edn. (Hauppauge, NY: Barrons Educational Series), p. 512.

amount of money available. Shall we discuss life insurance under the heading of insurance or of something called "capital accumulation?" If sellers give warranties, are they insurers?

The opening section of Spencer Kimball's casebook on insurance makes a fundamental point about the various definitions of insurance. There is no single definition which will work for all contexts and purposes.[26] The contexts in which insurance operates and has operated are so varied, and the institution itself exists in so many forms, that a comprehensive definition is essentially impossible. Kimball moves from this rejection of a single definition to a list of the typical insurance coverages of middle-class existence in this society, including of course the idea "at this time." Perhaps the question is not "what is insurance?" as if it is a word with one meaning, but something more like: how many meanings, and how large are the meanings, attached to the idea of insurance?[27] Spencer Kimball, in seeing clearly that the issue between the European and American perspectives on the subject had precisely to do with the issue of the involvement of government, saw also the tendency of the American professional discussion to focus on a narrow definition. He noted that in 1959, representatives of the industry could argue against the use of the word insurance for government pension plans.[28]

The question how is insurance distinguishable from investment or saving—is this self-insurance?—or from warranty[29]—becomes important because of the American (technical) approach to insurance. It is also important if we examine the rhetoric of insurance. Certain definitions may eliminate large issues, as when a short nineteenth-century discussion of the morality of life insurance says "life insurance is an investment of funds for the benefit of heirs, it is nothing more or less."[30]

---

26 Spencer Kimball (1962), *Insurance Law*. (Boston, MA: Little, Brown). See also Lawrence Friedman (1969), "Social Welfare Legislation: An Introduction," *Stanford Law Review* 21, 217–47 (discussing definitional problems in terms like "social legislation" or "social insurance").

27 This subject might be engaged comparatively. "The theoretical treatment of insurance in American economic literature differs from that in European, particularly German, literature. Many outstanding American writers consider insurance as only one of the numerous risk covering agencies and therefore give inadequate or primarily legalistic definitions of its functions. Elsewhere this point of view is not generally held; with Germany as its center of growth, insurance has developed as an independent discipline distinct from other fields of economics and as such has received separate and extensive treatment," Edward Seligman and Alvin Johnson (eds) (1937), *Encyclopaedia of the Social Sciences* (New York: Macmillan), p. 95.

28 See Spencer L. Kimball (1961), "The Purpose of Insurance Regulation: A Preliminary Inquiry in the Theory of Insurance Law", *Minnesota Law Review* 45, 471–524, pp. 512–13.

29 Either one of which would reduce the injury from an unanticipated accident for the person injured or government benefits.

30 Brewster (1850), "The Morality of Life Insurance," *Hunts Merchant Magazine and Commercial Review* 22, January, p. 117.

The need for historical work on insurance is as obvious now as it was when Kimball addressed the issue several decades ago, referring to the need for state-by-state inquiry in the American context.[31] William Vance, in 1904, referred to 30,000 cases in "English print" on the subject of insurance.[32] And now? Comparative insights also suggest complexities. There are other questions that might be explored comparatively. Ewald's description of the solidarity paradigm identified with the welfare state fits some countries in the world, but as suggested, the United States may not be among them. The language of solidarity is itself odd when used to describe American society. Insurance as solidarity is, in the United States, an idea that may reflect the historic connections between industrial insurance and the labor movement. It seems artificial with reference to the contemporary use of insurance by the middle class (the class that is the subject of Kimball's list of various kinds of insurances, in his insurance casebook).[33] Insurance may seem less a matter of solidarity than a matter of class-status maintenance for individuals. The demand for *Total Justice* (the suggestive title of Lawrence Friedman's book), includes the demand for long and healthy life, and perfect and perfectly formulated infants and may thus reflect a continuing commitment to the scientific utopian model.[34] But we also see something else in America. Science and technology are widely understood as having incalculable side effects. The risk of becoming uninsurable, through, for example, early detection of cancer, may be as great a risk for the middle class as the risk of unemployment or accident.

If we consider the seller's warranty on a product, we could easily think that the buyer was somehow insured against injury by the seller. But the transaction seems to omit the critical element in those definitions of the insurance transaction that stresses risk by a group of people, all of whom might be injured unexpectedly in the same way. That a legal contract can be a foundation for formal communitarianism seems clear.[35] The basic American understanding of insurance is that it is a contract, and, moreover, a contract with a commercial insurance company,[36] which also involves

---

31 See Kimball, *Insurance Law*. In addition to Kimball's work, see Lawrence Friedman (1965), *Contract Law in America.* (Madison, WI: University of Wisconsin Press), pp. 61–9 (discussing insurance law).

32 William Reynolds Vance (1904), *Handbook on the Law of Insurance* (St Paul, MN: West), Preface.

33 See Spencer Kimball, *Insurance Law*, p. xxv.

34 See Lawrence Friedman (1985), *Total Justice* (New York: Russell Sage Foundation).

35 See Carol Weisbrod (1980), *The Boundaries of Utopia* (New York: Pantheon).

36 This emphasis on contract is clear in a description of insurance given in *Holland Jurisprudence*, T.E. Holland (1880) (Oxford: Clarendon Press): "Insurance is a contract by which one party, in consideration of a premium, engages to indemnify another against a contingent loss, by making him a payment in compensation if, or when, the event shall happen by which the loss is to accrue" (p. 200) The company appears pervasively, e.g. "Adverse Selection: process in life insurance by which an applicant who is uninsurable, or is a greater than average risk, seeks to obtain a policy from a company at a standard premium rate. Life insurance companies carefully screen applicants for this reason, since their premiums are

other people, and even creates a certain relationship between them to the extent that they are sharers of a common risk and must pay in one same category.[37] Still, the word is used loosely, as when Elizabeth Warren notes that "a stay-at-home mother served as the ultimate insurance against unemployment or disability—insurance that added economic stability to the family, insurance that had a very real economic value even when it wasn't drawn on."[38] Warren notes that saving the second income might reduce the risk that the threats were doubled when both adults work, but then notes that the savings rate in the United States has doubled. Does not that make the point that advertising drives the level of consumption up; assumes that fear of class drop does it—true—but not unaided. Further, it seems that the amount of the insurance—the wages of an unskilled worker—would sometimes not be enough to maintain middle-class status.

Adam Feibelman argues that bankruptcy has a social insurance function, whether analyzed in terms of economic theory (risk transfer for a price) or functionally as a general measure of protection.[39]

As noted, the history of insurance is going to be different in different countries. It should presumably be connected to the history of commerce, generally.[40]

For Francois Ewald, writing about France, a critical date is 1898, when the adoption of a French scheme of insurance for industrial accidents ushered in the modern age. Following an emphasis on assistance in the form of charity, France[41] moved to a regime that Ewald described in terms of solidarity. "The paradigm of *solidarity*, which corresponds to the welfare state, considerably extends the proportion of legal obligations." These legal obligations tend to overlap moral obligations. Solidarity,

---

based on policyholders in average good health and in non-hazardous occupations." Rubin, *Barron's Dictionary of Insurance Terms*, p. 17.

37 And again, "a contract of insurance is an agreement in which one party (the insurer), in exchange for a consideration provided by the other party (the insured), assumes the other party's risk and distributes it across a group of similarly situated persons, each of whose risk has been assumed in a similar transaction". Jerry, *Understanding Insurance Law*, p. 17.

38 Elizabeth Warren (2004), "New Economics of the American Family", *American Bankruptcy Institute Law Review* 12, 1–48, p. 4.

39 Adam Feibelman (2005), "Defining the Social Insurance Function of Consumer Bankruptcy", *American Bankruptcy Institute Law Review* 13, 129–86.

40 On religious objections to commerce in the ancient world, see Jacob Viner (1972), *The Role of Providence in the Social Order: An Essay in Intellectual History* (Philadelphia, PA: American Philosophical Society): "Commerce by ships was itself an impious activity … an affront to providence, which intended the seas to be barriers to the contact of peoples …", p. 34. He traces the development of the pro-commerce position found in a religious form as late as 1894: "God made this world so that every nation in it has got to depend for something upon some other nation," p. 40.

41 François Ewald (1999), "The Return of the Crafty Genius", *Connecticut Insurance Law Journal* 6: 47–80 describes the relationship between the paradigms.

as Ewald sees it, involves "a sort of general right to compensation when faced with any mishap of living."[42]

It is far from clear that this is a description of the United States. At the simplest level, the time frame in the United States would be different. In the United States, in 1901, relief from mining accidents was conceived within the context of private charity. A book on the Scofield Utah Mine disaster, which took place in 1900, makes plain the private locus of social responsibility:

> Benefit. Published by authority of the Rathbone Lodge No. 9, Knights of Pythias of Scofield, and Scofield Lodge No 32, I.O.O.F, of Scofield, Utah, for the benefit of the Widows and Orphans, left alone and fatherless, to fight life's battles, unaided by the advice of husband or father.[43]

While some discussion merges state and private insurance in a general idea of the "risk society," other discussions, and perhaps particularly American discussions, keep these elements separate.

---

42 Ewald, "The Return of the Crafty Genius". "It is contemporary with a scientific and technical utopia, where society would have the possibility of controlling itself, where knowledge would have an indeterminate control over power. In its philosophical foundations, it is inseparable from the imperative of prevention: prevention of illnesses (with Pasteur's discoveries), prevention of crimes (with the system of social defense), prevention of accidents (with the sciences of safety), prevention of poverty and social insecurity (with social insurances)" p. 48.

43 The Scofield Mine Disaster. Public officials sent condolences. A researcher looking for a commemorative wrote that "sympathy and charity poured into stricken families." LaVerne Stallings (1959), "The Scofield Mine Disaster", *Western Folklore*, Vol. 18, No. 2, 173–6, p. 173. For a brief treatment of the American approaches in the 1960s, see Theodore J. Lowi "Risks and Rights in the History of American Government", in Edward J. Burger (ed.) *Risk*, (1993) (Ann Arbor: University of Michigan Press) pp. 17–40. But it seems that even the expansion of the welfare state and social programs in the United States through the Great Society period would not result in a description of the sort that the European sociologists are taking as their point of reference. Lawrence Friedman's characterization of workman's compensation as a "compromise" makes the basic point. (Friedman, *History of American Law*, 2nd edn. (New York: Simon & Schuster, p. 8).

On the theme of American exceptionalism compare James Harrington Boyd (1913), *A Treatise on the Law of Compensation for Injuries to Workmen Under Modern Industrial Statutes* (Indianpolis, IN: Bobbs Merrill), p. 16 ("Every civilized nation in Europe and many other nations in other parts of the world except the United States have discarded the old system of Employer's Liability based upon fault and substituted a system under which every industry bears the burden of relieving the distress caused by injuries to workers in any given industry practically without litigation.") with Barry R. Furrow, Thomas L. Greaney, Sandra H. Johnson, Timothy Jost and Robert L. Schwartz (1995), *Health Law*, Vol. 2. (St Paul, MN: West), Chapters 11–end, p. 102. ("Unlike virtually every other industrialized nation, the United States has not, as of this writing, developed a program for making health care comprehensively available to its citizens.")

Vance, for example, clearly distinguished the two in his treatment of the German efforts and their possible applicability to the American situation. "These experiments in Europe are being tried along the same lines as those pursued by the larger corporations" in the United States, Vance said. These experiments "may well be watched by us with great interest, with a view to their extension by corporate employers, and possibly to the ultimate adoption of such insurance as a governmental function."[44]

And Vance's introductory remarks make plain that insurance is, in his view, a theory that can be put into practice by any institution: "The student must observe that there is no reason why a contract of insurance shall not be made in any case where an actual loss may be suffered." Vance indicated that whatever the contract may be called, or through whatever agencies it may be made, or whatever other incidents it may have associated with it, the agreement is still one of insurance, and subject to the rules of insurance law, if the requisite elements are present."[45] If one tries to tell the history through time, one runs up against the serious definitional problem identified by Vance in his essay on the early history of insurance: shall we take the broad reimbursement ideas of the ancient trading societies as the start of insurance, or shall we restrict ourselves to a more modern understanding based on risk and risk spreading?[46] Shall we adopt for historical research the distinction offered by Ulrich Beck, between pre-industrial dangers, and "risk," defined now as the result of industrially related decisions, so that risk is defined as "modern?"[47] Shall we follow the lead of Mary Douglas and assume that perceptions of risk are culturally specific,[48] or expand some suggestions in Giddens, that, as rooted in trust, they may also be individually specific?[49] And if we decide to research insurance through a focus on the "modern" or "post-modern", where shall we begin? In what country? In what legal system? Under what ideological (including theological) frameworks?

44 See Vance, *Handbook on the Law of Insurance*, pp. 25–6.

45 The description of government efforts in the 1951 edition of Vance, *Handbook on the Law of Insurance*, seems less open about the Government effort.

46 William Reynolds Vance (1909), "Early History of Insurance", in *Anglo American Legal Essays* 100 pp. 98-116.

47 See Ulrich Beck (1992), *Towards a New Modernity* (trans. Mark Ritter) (London, Newbury Park, CA; Sage), p. 21.

48 Mary Douglas and Aaron Wildavsky (1983) *Risk and Culture* (Berkeley: University of California Press).

49 Anthony Giddens' discussion of ontological insecurity and trust includes reference to R.D. Laing and Erickson. Anthony Giddens (1990), *The Consequences of Modernity*, p. 92.

Insurance as a Contract of Community

In the writings of the American philosopher Josiah Royce, we find a stress on the point that "the greatest social power" of insurance "depends upon the fact that a man does not in general purchase an insurance policy merely for the transient creature of today called 'himself.'"[50] Rather, a man purchases insurance for his 'beneficiary.' "The beneficiaries may include people or corporations of whose very existence he, the individual, is little aware. But his linkages with such beneficiaries may join him to the whole social order."[51] Life insurance, perhaps all insurance, should be well-regarded for this reason. Yet, a certain ambivalence may continue to be entertained about insurance, including life insurance, by quite mainstream religious groups. The Lutheran Encyclopedia article on insurance is positive along conventional lines, arguing for insurance as a way to protect loved ones. But it ends on a quite different note: "A warning: The Christian remains mindful of the fact that all forms of material security have their limitations and that they dare not become a form of idolatry. Ultimately the believer entrusts his material as well as his spiritual and eternal security to God."[52]

Harold Kushner's treatment of insurance in *When Bad Things Happen to Good People* begins with the position that insurance ultimately cannot compensate for the true, emotional, non-financial loss.[53] In short, financial compensation at its best is not enough. We are not indifferent between the thing or person (lost or injured) and the financial equivalent of what we have lost.

Another comment on insurance relates to the practice of the companies in discussing natural disasters as Acts of God. Kushner suggests that these are simply events in nature.[54] It is the human cooperation after the disaster that is the act of God.

It is not only the radical separatists, like the Amish who worry about certain tendencies that insurance might intensify; beyond this, there is a conception of insurance and its limitations, which is focused quite differently, largely on political and communitarian issues. If certain objections to insurance, whether public or private, rest on the idea that it is in conflict with the idea of obedience to divine will, or undercuts the impact of divine judgment, a different idea sees insurance as a way of "bearing each other's burdens" and fostering community.

One way to consider insurance conceives it as an extension of family and particularly an extension of the family contract discussion. Insurance is the creation

---

50 Josiah Royce (1969), *The Basic Writings of Josiah Royce* (ed. John J. McDermott), 2nd edition. (Chicago: University of Chicago Press), p. 1136.

51 Ibid.

52 E.C. Knorr (1965), "Insurance", in Julius Bodensieck (ed.) *Encyclopedia of the Lutheran Church* (for the Lutheran World Federation) (Minneapolis, MN: Augsburg), p. 1152.

53 See generally Harold S. Kushner (1981), *When Bad Things Happen to Good People* (New York: Schocken).

54 See ibid., p. 59.

of a very large family through contract. Several insurance companies describe themselves in fact as families. The relationship is seen, however, as one between the company and the insured, which is the way a modern lawyer or economist tends to see it. If we pursue the family or community idea, the relationship is one that binds the insured together.

The utopian idea has a clear connection to fraternal organizations as providers of insurance, as it does to the history of immigration and the attempts by social agencies to assist them. Both the insurance agent and the "friendly visitor"[55] (as well, one assumes, as the parish priest) visited the homes of the poor.[56]

But it is also linked to the history of these independent insurance companies that stressed service goals. A report from the Metropolitan Life Insurance Company in 1914 indicates that, for that enterprise at least, the Temple of Insurance image suggested by the architecture of its New York office had substance.[57] It was reflective of a program of activities, some directed to employees, some to policyholders, some to the general community, which went far beyond our idea of a relationship based on the contractual obligation to pay claims. Metropolitan's newsletter was published in many languages. The company was proud of its general circulation library. Metropolitan sponsored a tuberculosis hospital for outreach public health programs. The tone of the 1914 volume is optimistic, progressive, paternalistic. Even the Armstrong inquiry and the New York insurance commissioner had good things to say about Metropolitan Life. But not all solidarity or associated ideas end with either religion or communitarianism. D.R. Jacques' formulations of 1849 relate to the expanded list of risks that insurance might cover, enlarged[58] but still finite, creating a contrast between insurance and Fourier and the socialists.[59] Jacques' position, that one must begin with things as they are, is a clear statement of a reformist position: "if society needs something more effectual than the forms of civil government, and the guarantees of civil liberty" to secure the welfare of the masses, it also needs something more feasible than new theories of society.[60]

---

55 Mary Wilcox Brown (1899), *The Development of Thrift* (New York: Macmillan), including a discussion of the "friendly visitor.").

56 See Walter Nichols (1909), "Fraternal Life Insurance", in Lester Zartman (ed.) (1921–23), *Yale Readings on Insurance*, 2nd edition, (New Haven: Yale University Press) p. 132.

57 See Metropolitan Life Insurance Company (1914), "Metropolitan Life Insurance Company Report, Its History, Its Present Position in the Insurance World, Its Home Office Building and Its Work Carried on Therein", New York, p. 30.

58 See also John D. Long (1971), *Ethics, Morality, and Insurance: A Long-Range Outlook.* (Bloomington, IN: Bureau of Business Research, Indiana University), p. 264, n. 36 (referring to an expanded list, including "bizarre" idea of divorce insurance).

59 D.R. Jacques (1849), "Society on the Basis of Mutual Life Insurance", *Hunt's Merchants' Magazine* 16, 152–3 (discussed in Tom Baker (1996), *On the Genealogy of Moral Hazard*, *Texas Law Review* 75, 237–92, n. 38.

60 Ibid.

Jacques' basic attack was on these new theories of society. He seems to be a social conservative. (Tom Baker contrasts his position to that of Karl Marx. Where Jacques wanted solidarity through risk sharing, Marx wanted collective ownership.) Jacques echoes a line for which we often cite DeToqueville. "The great and growing inclination to associated action which pervades society in this age, has been often remarked."[61] The associated action takes the form of partnerships, "incorporation, joint stock companies, lodges, and clubs." And of course "the principle of associated action" has also done a good deal for insurance.[62] Jacques urges that these facts force us to consider this question: "May not this plan, which has done so much in the form of insurance, do far more by means of insurance?" Insurance "does not pretend to diminish the aggregate of human misfortunes," Jacques said.[63] Rather, "it assumes that aggregate amount as a fixed fact." But it also assumes the larger aggregate of prosperity as equally certain. Insurance "presents society a union for mutual aid, of the fortunate and unfortunate, where those only who need it receive aid, and those only who can afford it are put to expense." Even then if it is true that suffering is undiminished and uncertainty continues to exist, still the aggregate of "human ingenuity and co-operation equalize the distribution of this fearful aggregate, and alleviate the terrors of uncertainty."[64]

Spencer Kimball noted as a feature of German insurance history that it referred to an "insured community" in "a most mystical" term.[65] Yet there are ways in which the links between insurance and community, the community of insured, are highly problematic. If it is a community, then it is one radically different from those that saw themselves as sharing beliefs or ethnicities and offering protection to those affiliated.[66]

Clearly the values of community can be seen as sustained by insurance. But for others, the idea of mutual aid and community meant rejection of all forms of insurance, public and private.

---

61 Ibid.

62 Ibid.

63 Ibid. For an argument that insurance changes perceptions of misfortune and consequences, see Deborah Stone, "Beyond Moral Hazard". Insurance, to the extent that it is an enforcer of mechanisms of safety, might be seen as reducing the aggregate of misfortune.

64 Ibid.

65 Spencer L. Kimball (1961), "The Purpose of Insurance Regulation: A Preliminary Inquiry in the Theory of Insurance Law", *Minnesota Law Review* 45, 471–525, pp. 471–7, n.35.

66 Here, the risk is expulsion. See Frederick L. Hoffman, (1900) *History of the Prudential*, (Newark NJ, Prudential Press) p. 7 quoting Sidney Webb on fraternal insurance: "A member who has paid a whole life-time to the sick and superannuation funds may at any moment be expelled and forfeit all claims for reasons quite unconnected with his desire for insurance in old age. Against the decision of his fellow-members there is in no case any appeal; moreover, the scale of contributions and benefits may at any time be altered even to the extent of abolishing the benefits altogether; and such alterations do, in fact, even take place in spite of all the protests of the minorities of old members."

Dystopian Aspects of Insurance

The history of the Mennonites and insurance captures the essentials of the argument opposing insurance. An account in the *Mennonite Encyclopedia* explains that opposition to life insurance was originally very strong, with excommunication as the sanction. "Applicants for membership were required to surrender their insurance policies before being received."[67] This opposition covered all forms of insurance, but by the beginning of the twentieth century, "opposition to fire and auto accident insurance had greatly diminished."[68] Workmen's compensation "created serious problems for conservative Mennonites at first, but ultimately this was generally accepted."[69]

Eventually, even the absolute prohibition on life insurance was changed, with only certain parts of the denomination prohibiting it altogether. Finally:

> in the General Conference Mennonite Church, the Mennonite Brethren Church, and certain related groups, whatever minor opposition there once may have been has completely disappeared, although such opposition apparently never was very strong.[70]

The Mennonite opposition to insurance had several dimensions. They believed that "it reflects trust in man rather than in God";[71] and it meant becoming "unequally yoked together with unbelievers";[72] insurance was "equivalent to merchandising in human life";[73] it is putting a monetary price on human life, which is considered unscriptural since man is the "temple of the Holy Ghost ..."[74]

Further, many Mennonites "also objected to taking out life insurance because it was contrary to the spirit of genuine mutual aid and brotherhood"[75] and finally, "the corrupt practices of many earlier life insurance companies were often cited as objections to all life insurance."[76] The corrupt history of the industry "greatly fortified the theological arguments."[77]

---

67 *The Mennonite Encyclopedia: A Comprehensive Reference Work on the Anabaptist Mennonite Movement*, (1955-1990) (eds C.J. Dyck and D.D. Martin) (Hillsboro, Kansas: Mennonite Brethren Publishing House, p. 343.

68 Ibid.

69 Ibid.

70 Ibid.

71 Ibid.

72 Ibid., p. 344.

73 Ibid.

74 Ibid.

75 Ibid.

76 Ibid.

77 Ibid. One American court wrote in the late nineteenth century: "Some companies, chartered by the legislature as insurance companies, were organized for the purpose of providing one or two of their officers, at head-quarters, with lucrative employment—large compensation for light work—not for the purpose of insuring property; for the payment of expenses, not of losses." *Delancy v. Insurance Co.*, 52 NH 581 (NH 1873). It may be noted,

This article in *The Mennonite Encyclopedia* then goes on to describe forms of mutual aid within the group. "A form of mutual brotherly aid insurance has developed among Mennonites in North America in recent decades in the form of death and burial and benefit associations, which are in effect life insurance arrangements."[78] Nonetheless, the position is that these are substantially and significantly different from ordinary insurance. Five factors are listed: (1) the benefit payments are small, intended to cover only the cost of the burial,[79] or also medical bills attendant upon the last illness; (2) the system is entirely and truly mutual; (3) salary payments to officials are non-existent or very low; (4) no agents' premiums are paid; (5) membership is limited to church members.[80]

Another idea that results in the rejection of insurance is based not on mutual aid but on self-reliance. Here is Gandhi's discussion:

> About the time I took up chambers in Bombay, an American insurance agent had come there—a man with a pleasing countenance and a sweet tongue. As though we were old friends he discussed my future welfare. "All men of your status in America have their lives insured. Should you not also insure yourself against the future? Life is uncertain. We in America regard it as a religious obligation to get insured. Can I not tempt you to take out a small policy?"

Gandhi's responses are both thoughtful and emphatic.

> Up to this time I had given the cold shoulder to all the agents I had met in South Africa and India, for I had thought that life assurance implied fear and want of faith in God. But now I succumbed to the temptation of the American agent. As he proceeded with his argument, I had before my mind's eye a picture of my wife and children. "Man, you have sold almost all the ornaments of your wife," I said to myself. "If something were to happen to you, the burden of supporting her and the children would fall on your poor brother, who has so nobly filled the place of father. How would that become you?" With these and similar arguments I persuaded myself to take out a policy for Rs. 10,000.

He records then that in South Africa his life and his views changed.

> All the steps I took at this time of trial were taken in the name of God and for His service. I did not know how long I should have to stay in South Africa. I had a fear that I might never be able to get back to India; so I decided to keep my wife and children with me and earn enough to support them. This plan made me deplore the life policy and feel ashamed of having been caught in the net of the insurance agent. If, I said to myself, my brother is really in the position of my father, surely he would not consider it too much of a burden to support my widow, if it came to that. And what reason had I to assume that death would claim me earlier than the others? After all, the real protector was neither I, nor my

---

however even this can be defined as an aspect of community of a particular social class. See Anthony F.C. Wallace (1980), *Rockdale* (New York: Norton), pp. 49–50.

78 *The Mennonite Encyclopedia* (1957), p. 344.

79 Life insurance may be conceived as burial insurance at times.

80 See *The Mennonite Encyclopedia* (1957), at 344.

brother, but the Almighty. In getting my life insured I had robbed my wife and children of their self-reliance. Why should they not be expected to take care of themselves? What happened to the families of the numberless poor in the world? Why should I not count myself as one of them? A multitude of such thoughts passed through my mind, but I did not immediately act upon them. I recollect having paid at least one insurance premium in South Africa.[81]

The manipulations of insurance are familiar in fiction, both in the many stories which involve murder for insurance and in stories by writers known more as moralists than as detective writers, e.g. Brecht, who saw insurance as one more way for the world to reduce the humanity of individuals. Brecht's story involved the manipulation of the appearance of health in the insured to change the selling price of the policy to new buyers.[82] Another writer not known as an insurance specialist, Robert Heinlein, used the uncertainty aspect of insurance as the theme of his first story, on life insurance.[83]

Some aspects of the insurance enterprise can be viewed as dystopian. This section reviews several of these. It focuses on the exclusion of the uninsurable; the artificial nature of the community of the insured; the idea that insurance companies want people to buy insurance and also want not to pay claims and the related tendency of the insurance industry to focus on the darker more deceitful side of human nature. One writer said:

> It may seem unkind to a candidate to be rejected as a "bad" life, but Insurance Companies are commercial undertakings, not charitable societies. If insurance were universal, Companies would probably be quite willing to abolish the medical examination and provide insurance protection for all ranks and conditions of men. As it is, they are obliged to discriminate between good and bad lives; and an Office is successful in proportion to the care with which it accepts lives. Let us drop the subject.[84]

At the heart of modern insurance there is a decision about inclusion and exclusion that cuts against the idea of mutual aid as understood by those groups that define themselves in terms other than insurability. For such groups, insurability is a consequence of inclusion in the group. Exclusion from the group results in withdrawal of mutual aid. Here, too, we may see the function of social control as described in some recent work.[85] To the extent that utopian goals are viewed as desirable, it

---

81 Mohandas K. Gandhi, *Autobiography: The Story of My Experiments with Truth* (trans. Mahadev Desai) (New York: Dover Publications), pp. 230–31. The idea of the support projected from the brother gets us back to Kirksey.

82 Bertolt Brecht (1998), "A Little Tale of Insurance", in Bertolt Brecht, *Collected Short Stories*, (New York: Arcade Publishing), pp. 90–93.

83 Heinlein, (1098[1939]) "Life-line", in Robert Heinlein *Expanded Universe* (New York: Penguin Putnam), pp. 5–27, p. 4.

84 Arthur Reade (1905), *The Story of Life Insurance*, (Manchester: Hotspur Press) p. 44.

85 See, for example, Pat O'Malley (1998), "Imagining Insurance Risk: Thrift and Industrial Life Insurance in Britain", *Connecticut Insurance Law Journal* 5, 675–706.

becomes necessary to shape people so that they are within the average risk pool, people who avoid hazardous activity and whose behavior generates good health. It is only through coercion that they can be insurable.[86]

Those who were uninsurable were excluded from the group because of their uninsurability. This was one of the reasons the Mennonites gave for their objections to insurance. Their objections to insurance were bolstered by a "powerful practical argument, namely, that the commercial insurance companies did not really help the needy, but sought only to protect the health and rejected as poor risks the weak and the ill who really needed protection."[87] The Mennonites considered it a practical, rather than religious argument. But it seems to have theoretical aspects if we say that it is the existence of the excluded which makes possible happiness of the others.[88]

The image of insurance in connection to the social order is evident in general discussions of the function of the state. Thus, John Finnis notes that: "political community exists partially (and sometimes primarily) as a kind of business arrangement between self-interested associates." (This, however, was "the kind of mutual insurance association or "social contract" derided by Aristotle and all the classics for its meagerness as a form [or account] of community.")[89]

86 Compare Richard Titmuss (1959), *Essays on the Welfare State*, pp. 66–67: "The long-term and foreseeable dependencies of old age—should be shouldered by progressive taxation just as the long-term dependencies of childhood are." See also Peter T. Kilborn (1999) "Tennessee Talks of Paring Plan for Uninsurables", *New York Times*, May 1, Section A, p. 1, column 2 (discussing uninsurability in state context).

87 *The Mennonite Encyclopedia* (1957) p. 344.

88 See William James (1956[1897]), *The Will to Believe* (Mineola: Dover), p. 188: " … [I]f the hypothesis were offered us of a world in which Messrs. Fourier's and Bellamy's and Morris's utopias should all be outdone, and millions kept permanently happy on the one simple condition that a certain lost soul on the far-off edge of things should lead a life of lonely torture, what except a special and independent sort of emotion can it be which would make us immediate feel, even though an impulse arose within us to clutch at the happiness so offered, how hideous a thing would be its enjoyment when deliberately accepted as the fruit of such a bargain?"). See also Ursula K. Le Guin, "The Ones who Walk Away from Omelas," in *The Wind's Twelve Quarters* (New York: Harper & Row), pp. 224–31. She describes this as "variations on a theme by William James," Le Guin (1975), *The Wind's Twelve Quarters*, p. 275.

Another version of the exclusions of insurance is suggested by Ulrich Beck, who, as previously noted, uses the term "risk" to mean controllable limited calculable and then insurable and risk and the word "threat" to refer to global meta threats. The line between the minor technical risk and the threat or hazard is, finally, established by the market, through the question of what will be insured by commercial insurance companies.

89 John Finnis (1991), *Natural Law*, (Aldershot, Dartmouth) p. 149. Finnis quotes Aristotle to the effect that "the *polis* was formed not for the sake of life only but rather for the good life" … "it does not exist [merely] for the sake of trade and of business relations … any *polis* which is truly so called, and is not one merely in name, must devote itself to the aim of encouraging excellence [*arete*]."

In the current discussion, uncertainty—at least as experienced by some people—is the central theme of insurance. "Under the present capitalistic organization of society," Edward Woods wrote in 1928, "there are certain risks which every individual must face in everyday life, the untimely incidence of any one of which might transform him from a self-supporting producer in comfortable circumstances to-day into a dependent cripple or pauper to-morrow."[90] The emphasis must be on the untimeliness of the risk as much as the risk itself, so that life insurance is linked to the idea of premature death of the wage earner, since the fact of death is certain. The reduction of the risks of life is linked to a story of the expansion of rights and control over the future.

Another aspect of insurance that has received attention is its normative effect on behavior.[91] If insurance companies will reduce rate for certain behaviors, those are encouraged. If not, those behaviors are discouraged. In an early example of fire insurance, the first Lord Mayor of London rules [in 1189] that all houses have to be equipped with a ladder and, during tinder-dry summers, a barrel of water by the front door.[92] This is also an early example of the way in which modern insurance advances substantive goals. Moreover, those goals may be perceived as being as indistinguishable from state goals as from state sanctions. When people say that they can't stay in a hospital longer than two days, they are using a formulation more appropriate for the criminal law. They "can't"; are not allowed to. What they mean, more precisely, is that a company will not reimburse.

As to this normative regulation, companies may be right or wrong in the connections that they see between particular behavior and risk reduction. Their guess may be common sense, or statistical analysis, or pseudo-statistical analysis. Their determination of rates may involve redlining, which is for other reasons considered inappropriate. In all these cases, they are operating as a powerful private government.

Ewald has noted that as a society becomes secularized, the orientation of a speaker associated with the general social orientation here has less to do with God or morals as with ethics. Thus, in discussing the current cautionary paradigm, he writes that:

> The new paradigm of *safety* ... bears witness to a deeply disturbed relationship to a science that is questioned less for the knowledge that it offers than for the doubts that it insinuates. Here, moral obligations take the shape of ethics, and the principle of responsibility is seen as a reflection of the new notion of *precaution*.[93]

---

90 Edward A. Woods (1928), *The Sociology of Life Insurance* (New York: Appleton), p. 1.

91 See Carol Heimer (2002), "Insuring More, Ensuring Less: The Benefits of Private Regulation through Insurance", in Baker and Simon *Embracing Risk*, pp. 116–45.

92 Stephen Mihm (1999), "Once Upon a Time, Only Kings had Clothes: Milestones, Millstones as Design Marches On", *New York Times*, December 30, p. F1, column 6.

93 François Ewald (1999), "The Return of the Crafty Genius: An Outline of a Philosophy of Precaution", *Connecticut Insurance Law Journal* 6, 47–80, p. 76. Ewald writes as to these

One idea is that the community created by actuarial insurance practices involves a distortion. Thus, Jonathan Simon has noted that "the shift toward actuarial practices alters the way we understand our status as subjects, both individual and group." Simon argues that "[b]y placing people in groups that have no experienced meaning for the members, and therefore lack the capacity to realize common goals or purposes, actuarial methods imply a particular view of individuals and their communities." The clear risk, as Jonathan Simon perceives it, is that people will understand themselves in terms of these representations "they may be stripped of a certain quality of belongingness to others that has long played a role in our culture."[94]

Insurance and an economic analysis can substitute one view of reality for another. Someone says "God is my insurer" and we call that person a "self-insurer." (But is it really substitution? Is it more like saying that a violin is a piece of wood? Another example of the contrast is between what others call you, what you call yourself, and what you are.)

To the extent that the insurance relationship is rooted in contract, it presents issues of commercialization and a potential flattening of human relationships similar to those debated in family law.[95] It is worth recalling that what is taken to be the first reference in an American law journal to the word "adhesion" is found in Patterson's article on life insurance,[96] published several years before Nathan Isaacs' well-known piece on adhesion contracts.[97] The contract emphasis resulted historically in an overreaching by insurance companies, followed by interventions by state authorities to protect the individual insured.[98] It is, in part, the contract's emphasis which makes possible the painful disparity between representations of insurance companies that relate to full security and fact of coverage of certain risks, and even then only under certain circumstances in accordance with the insurance contract.[99]

---

that they are not those worlds which succeed each other (responsibility replaced by solidarity replaced by precaution) but are rather "three attitudes with regard to uncertainty, assessed and developed at three moments in time" (p. 76).

94 Jonathan Simon (1988), "The Ideological Effects of Actuarial Practices", *Law & Society Review* 22, 771–800.

95 The family law discussion of contract and domestic relations is extensively reviewed in Schneider and Brinig (1996), *An Invitation to Family Law*, St. Paul, MN: West Publishing Company).

96 See Edwin W. Patterson (1919), "The Delivery of a Life-Insurance Policy", *Harvard Law Review* 33, 198–222 ("Life-insurance contracts are contracts of 'adhesion.'").

97 See Nathan Isaacs (1917), "The Standardizing of Contracts," *Yale Law Journal* 27, 34–48. That piece is treated as foundational on the subject of standard from contracts.

98 See the treatment of this question in Kessler and Gilmore, *Contracts* 627-34.

99 The legal perspective on insurance has for some time been reviewed in terms of the idea of contract. This contract optic is appropriate, whether we see that contract as one in which the risk holders have a stake in each other and have a contract with each other, or whether that contract is seen as a contract between individuals and insurance company.

The description Patterson offers of the life insurance purchase, a contractual transaction in which the buyer has no idea of what limits there are on what is being bought, remains important throughout the field, as it relates at least to consumers.

But an even more important point is that perhaps almost no one can understand the contract. This has implications for our judgment on the behavior of agents. "It is hard to accuse the agent of deliberate fraud," Lord Passfield (Sidney Webb) wrote. "He is perpetually driven—driven by the system itself, by the method by which he is paid, and by the ever-grinding pressure to replace lapses—to obtain a continual succession of new policies."[100] And "the people whom he has to canvass simply cannot understand the nature of the commodity that he is pressing them to purchase."[101] Finally, Lord Passfield asks, "[w]ho shall subsequently discover how much the agent actually said, how much he deliberately implied, and how much was honest misunderstanding that he suspected to exist, or was aware of, and merely neglected to dispel?"[102]

Even for professional buyers and sellers the insurance transaction is characterized, if not by gross disparity of bargaining power, at least by that willingness to put the details off until another day, which makes the "bargain," as in all standard form transactions, somewhat fictional. Then, too, there is the issue of the shifting "we" as used by the agent.

One answer suggests that this is not really a problem. Thus, it has been noted that perhaps: "the greatest source of ethical concern for many agents and brokers is the feeling that they are caught in the middle between two parties who have conflicting interests." The difficulty is that "on the one hand, an agent's primary responsibility is to serve the insurer." But it is also the case that the agent "owes, dedication, loyalty and service to the consumer." "How can an agent reconcile this conflict? Actually, it is quite simple. By acting in the best interests of the insurer, the agent best serves the consumer."[103]

Ambrose Bierce thought that "Insurance is 'An ingenious modern game of chance in which the player is permitted to enjoy the comfortable conviction that he is beating the man who keeps the table.'"[104] The view of the writer of *The Devil's Dictionary* has resonances. One might compare the comments of Mark Twain, in "An inquiry about Insurances," which takes the form of a conversation with an insurance agent. A man is told that a company has "issued over sixty thousand policies, forty-five of which have proved fatal and been paid for." He responded that the presentation reveals a problem. "You appear to have it pretty much all your own way, you see. It is all very well for the lucky forty-five that have died 'and been paid for,' but how

---

100 Sidney Webb (1915), "Passfield Report", *The New Statesman*, "Special Supplement on Industrial Insurance", IV: 101, p. 24 .

101 Ibid.

102 Ibid.

103 Rick Paszkiet (ed.) (1996), *Ethics for the Insurance Professional*, (Dearborn Financial Publishing), 2nd edition, p. 19.

104 Ambrose Bierce, *The Devils Dictionary*.

about the other fifty-nine thousand nine hundred and fifty-five?" The bottom line is "You have got their money, haven't you? but somehow the lightning don't seem to strike them and they don't get any chance at you."[105]

This argument, one of the two that Rubinow identified as the basic arguments against insurance, has particular force in relation to profit-making institutions. In pursuing his case for social insurance, Rubinow comments as to this point and as to the "moral hazard" argument, that one should assume for the sake of the discussion that they are true, and then go on to consider the benefits of insurance in terms of the security offered to those who will, in fact, suffer losses.[106]

A Complex Good

The idea of insurance carries a mixed message. On the one hand, one has the dictionary definitions of security and certainty (reinforced by the selling practices of the insurance companies themselves). On the other hand, there is the public image in which the insurance company signifies someone who will not pay a claim or will refuse to issue insurance to those who are seen to present risks too high—for example, battered wives.[107] The grim account of John Grisham's *The Rainmaker* reflects a common perception. It is not merely that there is a contractual argument in favor of the companies—that they have assumed only a particular responsibility under their contract—"it is that they are rich, untrustworthy, insensitive and corrupt."[108]

We can, perhaps, assume that the reputation of the insurance industry sometimes is a reflection of the industry's response to something real, a defect in human nature. In his short story "Hunted Down," Dickens wrote that "a Life Assurance Office is at all times exposed to be practiced upon by the most crafty and cruel of the human race."[109] Even Bob and Margaret on Comedy Central[110] are less than strictly honest in their approach to insurance. "When their house is burgled and it's time to fill

105 Mark Twain (1961), "An Inquiry about Insurance", in Charles Neider (ed.) *The Complete Humorous Sketches and Tales of Mark Twain*, pp. 78–80.

106 See I.M. Rubinow (1913), *Social Insurance*, p. 5; see also John H. Langbein and Bruce A. Wolk (1995), *Pensions and Employee Benefit Law*, (New York, Foundation) p. 4 (noting that Bismarck's scheme was not properly a pension system since it began at age 65, beyond what was then the normal life expectancy).

107 See Baker, *Containing the Promise of Insurance: Adverse Selection and Risk Classification*, Conn. Ins. L.J. 371–396 at 392.

108 See *The Rainmaker* (Paramount Pictures, 1998) (presenting a more hostile view of the insurance company than the book upon which the film is based).

109 Charles Dickens (1992), "Hunted Down", in Michael Cox (ed.) *Victorian Tales of Mystery and Detection* (Oxford: New York) pp. 46–68.

110 A television program about a dentist and his chiropodist wife, living in London, which aired in the United States on the cable station Comedy Central.

out the insurance forms, they enthusiastically list elaborate electronics they never owned."[111]

But are these aspects of human nature with which the companies must deal, manage or limit, or are they also a kind of resistance to the rationalizing tendencies of insurance?[112] Scott identified a number of leveling or flattening tendencies in early modern Western society, from maps of land to permanent family names, to census and population counts.[113] Max Weber stressed the significance of double entry bookkeeping.[114] Should the actuarial methods of insurance be added to this list?

Dominant associations with the idea of insurance are sometimes negative and critical. One criticism is that insurance is, in fact, dystopian. The security is seen as illusion, and the community as either non-existent or involving definitions of the group that defeat true solidarity. Insurance is seen as less a community and more a business—and a big business at that.[115] The criticism advanced by the Mennonites is not fixed on a marginal point. It is not about a particular debate over a detail about premiums or coverage (how much time in the hospital for maternity stays, for example). It is not an argument that certain kinds of transactions are intrinsically immoral, while the main enterprise is appropriate. Rather, the critique is focused on the fundamental concept that underlines the enterprise: the distinction between insurability and uninsurability and the related ideas of insurable risk and uninsurable risk.[116]

111 Anita Gates (1998), 'The New Seinfeld', *The Guardian*, July 10, p. 72. On another possible link between insurance and social deviance, see J. Owen Staltson (1942), *Marketing Life Insurance* (Cambridge: Harvard University Press), p. 660 (noting the suggestion that the beneficiary might sometimes be a "friend"); compare Tom Baker (1996), "On the Genealogy of Moral Hazard", *Texas Law Review* 75, 231–92 (discussing *Vanity Fair*, p. 252).

112 Not all scholars focus on issues of resistance. Foucault's work, as has been noted by Said and Walzer, is disinterested in this issue. See Michael Walzer (1986), "The Politics of Michel Foucault", in *Foucault, A Critical Reader* (Oxford: Blackwell), pp. 51–58; Edward W. Said (1986), "Foucault and the Imagination of Power", in David Couzens Hoy (ed.) *Foucault, A Critical Reader*, pp. 149–155.

113 James C. Scott (1998), *Seeing like a State* (New Haven: Yale University Press), pp. 87–8 (maps), 64–5, 66–7 (census).

114 Weber had defined his project as considering religious ideas as a cause of certain economic forms. Weber's book engendered much discussion as to the characterization of particular religions and their particular links to capitalist forms. The controversy tended to concede the legitimacy of the basic inquiry concerning relations between religion and economic development. See Anthony Giddens (1992), "Introduction", *The Protestant Ethic and The Spirit of Capitalism* (trans. Max Weber and Talcott Parsons) (New York: Routledge).

115 See generally Staltson, *Marketing Life Insurance*.

116 Definitions from a dictionary of insurance suggest the major point: "Underwriting: process of examining, accepting, or rejecting insurance risks, and classifying those selected, in order to charge the proper premium for each. The purpose of underwriting is to spread the risk among a pool of insureds in a manner that is equitable for the insureds and profitable for the insurer." *Barron's Dictionary of Insurance Terms*, p. 497. See also definitions of "risk management" and "risk selection," pp. 414–15. "Insurability: circumstance in which an

Our ambivalence towards insurances is captured in the odd tone of an advertisement by Mark Twain. When he was associated with an insurance company, he gave a speech containing the following paragraph:[117]

> I have seen an entire family lifted out of poverty and into affluence by the simple boon of a broken leg. I have had people come to me on crutches, with tears in their eyes, to bless this beneficent institution. In all my experience of life, I have seen nothing so seraphic as the look that comes into a freshly mutilated man's face when he feels in his vest pocket with his remaining hand and finds his accident ticket all right.

The paragraph is unsettling. Presumably the problem is the juxtaposition of the idea of mutilation with the picture a man patting his pocket to check on his policy. Is this Mark Twain as Ambrose Bierce? But the company reprinted the paragraph in a pamphlet. Is that because there is something in this uncomfortable juxtaposition that is true? That finally, it is better to be insured than to be uninsured?

The suggestion that a broken leg lifted a family out of poverty is explored further in another famous work that is essentially built on the same idea. Lorraine Hansberry, in *Raisin in the Sun*, wrote a play drawing on her family's experience with racial discrimination in housing.[118] And one might say that the play invokes legal institutions of property, restrictive covenants, and the rights of private ownership associations. But underneath the play as a whole is another legal institution, which is hardly mentioned at all, though it is the institution on which the entire play turns. The institution is insurance, and particularly life insurance, the policy payable to the beneficiary, here the widow, on the earth of the insured. The policy here is for 10,000—much more than a burial policy, and the play offers a description of the role of life insurance in providing capital for a class that had never known the possibility of capital. The 10,000 policy on Walter Younger's life, a policy bought with his blood, is the most money the family has ever seen, and opens the possibility of education, housing, business investment in a way that had never seemed realistic. The money is conceived roughly in thirds. One-third for the house in a white neighborhood, echo of *Hansberry v. Lee* (a case initiated by Lorraine Hansberry's father when she was a child), one-third for the education of a talented daughter, and one third for a son to use as he likes. The son trusts a faithless friend, and two-thirds of the money is effectively lost. But the one-third is a down payment on a house for a family for which a house, with a backyard, represents a major advance.[119] It is the life insurance policy that makes this possible.

---

insurance company can issue life or health insurance to an applicant based on standards set by the company." Ibid., p. 227.

117 Justin Kaplan (1966), *Mr. Clemens & Mark Twain* (New York: Simon & Schuster), p. 303.

118 See *Hansberry v. Lee*, 311 US 32 (1940).

119 Barbara Ehrenreich notes in *Nickeled and Dimed* that even the security deposit on an apartment requires some capital. Discussion of capital accumulation and insurance can also

The use of insurance in *Raisin in the Sun* makes plain the significance of the institution for the poorer parts of society. While it is clear enough that property insurance, for example, insures to the benefit of those who had property to begin with, life insurance here raised the possibility of capitalization for those who had never had it. The life insurance was designed to replace the wages of the head of the household. It does not quite operate that way because everyone else in the household works as well as the "head," and because saving alone, out of the modest incomes that the family brings home, would not have allowed the down payment on the house.

Then it is clear that religion has relevance to the story. But the accounts suggest certain methodological issues. To the extent that religious values are rooted in ancient texts or medieval interpretations, it is reasonable to ask whether these texts are to be understood as controlling in the same way over time and in all places. Perhaps, for example, the Canonist concern with usury in relation to insurance was not of particular importance in the nineteenth-century United States. Perhaps it can more usefully be related to the problem in twentieth-century Iran, where the Koranic injunctions against usurious contracts influence state law.[120] Issues of gambling, which in the nineteenth-century United States are understood in terms of frivolity and general immortality, may or may not retain an older association with divination. Clark, for example, relates gambling to the issues of knowing God's will, as do materials on Islamic law.[121]

Further, the idea that insurance goes against God's providence is an idea that has different components. For some, it is thought to be something that averts injury, in which case the twelfth-century precautions and safety devices are presumably vulnerable. For others, insurance is about mitigation, averting the consequences of the injury. The argument, against insurance is, for some, rebutted by a comparison to savings accounts, investment, umbrellas, as if the religious argument against life insurance assumed that the only appropriate religious stance is in effect quietism and passivity as one simply accepts that happens.[122] Some of the links to religion are visible as links, though their substance remains to be fully explored. What, for example, was the impulse behind the 1986 Connecticut Mutual study on societal religious values?[123] Would insurance companies have achieved their ideal condition when everyone could be covered by insurance because everyone was subject only to

---

focus on the participation of insurance companies in large capital markets. Baker, *Insurance Law and Policy*, pp. 10–11.

120 For discussion of Canonist and Jewish law approaches, see generally Stephen M. Passamanac (1974), *Insurance in Rabbinic Law* (Edinburgh: Edinburgh University Press).

121 See generally Geoffrey Clark (1999), *Betting on Lives* (Manchester: Manchester University Press).

122 See Walter B. Weare (1973), *Black Business in the New South* (Durham: Duke University Press), p. 87.

123 See on the general issues, John D. Long (1971), *Ethics, Morality, and Insurance* (Bloomington: Bureau of Business Research, Indiana University.

average risks?[124] What drives "social control" efforts by private insurance companies aimed at those outside their "community of insured?" Some of this activity may be about making the world less risky for their insured. Is some motivated by the idea of making those outside the existing community insurance-worthy?[125]

As the earlier discussion of the Mennonites makes plain, some groups may refuse insurance.[126] The modern Amish distinguish sometimes between liability insurance and other kinds of insurance. In one such discussion stressing issues of liability insurance, (insurance sometimes justified as "for the other person"), the writer says: "If Jesus were here today, can we imagine him worrying about his earthly possessions to the degree that he would have some insurance plan in case he had a loss?" The emphasis is on not worrying about the future unduly. Presumably it was right to worry some. In this discussion, insurance was on the wrong side of the line. It makes clear that the argument that insurance is the same as saving, or is simply another way of being careful and prudent does not answer the objection that some care is enough and other care is too much.[127] The issue of adaptations, when it arises at the national level, as in the case of Islamic states, may result in a variety of mechanisms to achieve the requisite objectives.[128] When it arises within a state that is not opposed to insurance in principle, it may either involve adaptations in the religious side[129] and/or requests for exemption from public insurance programs.

Within the American materials, the stance of the Amish on the insurance issue[130] is almost as well known as its position on the more familiar question of compulsory education. This results in a conversation on insurance between the religious group and the representatives of the larger society through the courts.[131]

---

124 The price of this might be high. Everyone average might mean everyone the same. But then mutual aid, among the utopians, e.g. Oneida, was sometimes joined to mutual criticism.

125 That is, insurable, as a way of fulfilling an unarticulated utopian-universalist goal and not merely by the desire to increase profits by increasing the number of buyers of insurance policies?

126 See generally Peter Ferrara (1993), "The Amish and Social Security", in Donald Kraybill (ed.) *The Amish and the State* (Baltimore: Johns Hopkins University Press) pp. 125–143 (presenting arguments of the Amish on insurance). Ideas of stewardship also have relevance here, since the position of the insured regarding property may not be the conventional one. Thus, in an Anabaptist discussion of dealing with what seems to be a delinquency issue, the question of responsibility to/for property is put in effect this way: What would God want his steward to do?

127 See Elmo Stoll (1984), "Is Insurance Right or Wrong", *Family Life* April, 8–11.

128 See Frank E. Vogel and Samuel L. Hayes (1998), *Islamic Banking, Islamic Law and Finance: Religion, Risk and Return* (Boston: Kluwer Law International), pp. 150–53.

129 For example, subjects of inquiry might include insurance in Islamic law and insurance in Jewish law.

130 See Brian J. Glenn (1999), "Collective Precommitment from Temptation: The Case of the Amish" *Rationality and Society* 13:2, 185–204.

131 For rejection of an individual's claim to a religious exception based on his "Christian beliefs," see *Bucklund v. Board of Commissioners of King County Hospital District No. 2*,

United States v. Lee held that an exemption for the Amish from the Social Security System was not constitutionally required.[132] The argument of the plaintiff in the case was built on an opposition to insurance on religious grounds, although as William Ball makes plain, the *Lee* case was not necessarily "an Amish case" in which a clear group position was at stake. "No Amish teachings has declared that the Amish religion forbade the payment of the employee's share of social security taxes."[133] The opinion by Justice Burger reviews the District Court opinion:

> Holding the statutes requiring the payment of social security and unemployment insurance taxes unconstitutional as applied. "The district court noted that the Amish believe it sinful not to provide for their own elderly and needy and therefore are religiously opposed to the national social security system."

The court also found that they reject state insurance, as well as commercial insurance, because of their religious commitments: "The Amish religion not only prohibits the acceptance of social security benefits, but also bars all contributions by Amish to the social security system."[134]

A footnote adds that, the Amishman complaining in *Lee* said that his scriptural basis for this belief was: "But if any provide not ... for those of his own house, he hath denied the faith, and is worse than an infidel" (I Timothy 5:8.).[135] Justice Burger commented on the Amish position, beginning with the point that while the statute mandated contributions it did not compel the acceptance of benefits. Thus, "it would be possible for an Amish member, upon qualifying for social security benefits, to receive and pass them along to an Amish fund having parallel objectives." But Justice Burger commented, "It is not for us to speculate whether this would ease or mitigate the perceived sin of participation."[136]

Justice Burger was, in effect, suggesting the possible use by the Amish of the sort of accommodation that makes insurance possible for other groups.

---

106 Wash. 2d 632, 633 (1986), *appeal dismissed*, 481 U.S. 1034 (1987) (upholding hospital's bylaws requiring doctors to carry professional liability insurance).

132 See *United States v. Lee*, 455 U.S. 252 (1982).

133 William Ball, "First Amendment Issues" in Donald B. Kraybill (ed.) (1993), *The Amish and the State*, p. 257. Ball, the attorney for the Amish in *Wisconsin v. Yoder*, 406 U.S. 205 (1972) in which the community won an exemption from two years of high school, suggests that Lee's position may not have represented the position of the judgment of the Amish bishops or a consensus of even his own Amish community. The Amish do not suggest that they themselves would necessarily find it impossible to contribute to social security without collecting it. Their stated concern in their legislative testimony was for ability of the next generation to resist temptation.

134 *Lee*, p. 255.

135 Note the direct invocation of a biblical authority, as against a discussion of authoritative interpretative material.

136 *Lee*, p. 261.

The Limits of Insurance

In the United States, the idea of progress suggested utopian goals rather than utopian achievements at the national level. It seems entirely possible that the aspiration of social insurance in America, from the New Deal forward, was not as wholehearted as those Ewald describes. The belief in salvation through science was perhaps not so completely pervasive. Ulrich Beck's description of a shift from a society of assumptions of knowability and certainty to one in which uncertainty has returned, may or may not describe America as a whole.[137] At the same time, what we do know may create problems for an insurance idea. Genetic testing, for example, may alter the risk basis of health insurance.[138]

We are aware of the irrationalities and failures of a world that we often call Kafkaesque. Tom Baker discusses the problem as an illustration of the ways in which precaution can increase rather than decrease risk.[139] It is appropriate, therefore, to end this section with a reference to material by Franz Kafka when he was working as a clerk at the Accident Insurance Institute in Prague on precisely this sort of question.

The annual report for the Institute is included by Max Brod in his biography of Kafka.[140]

Kafka was considering the "difference between square spindles and cylindrical spindles as it affects the technique for the prevention of accidents."[141] He described the machinery in some detail. "The cutters of the square spindle are connected by means of screws direct to the spindle and rotate with exposed cutting edges at speeds

137 See generally Ulrich Beck (1994), "The Reinvention of Politics: Towards a Theory of Reflexive Modernization", in Ulrich Beck, Anthony Giddens, Scott Lash (eds) *Reflexive Modernization: Politics, Tradition and Aesthetics in the Modern Social Order*. (Stanford, CA: Stanford University Press, p. 1.

138 Roberta Berry (1996), "The Human Genome Project and the End of Insurance", *University of Florida Journal of Law and Public Policy*, Vol. 7, 205–256, p. 206. See also Richard Ericson and Aaron Doyle (2004) *Uncertain Business: Risk, Insurance, and the Limits of Knowledge* (Toronto: Toronto University Press).

139 Tom Baker (2004), "Insuring Liability Risks", *Geneva Papers on Risk and Insurance* 29, 128–49.

140 See Max Brod (1960), 2nd edn *Franz Kafka: A Biography* (trans. Roberts and Winston) (New York: Schocken Books) pp. 82–3. Brod provides this account of the 1909 document: "The annual report of the accident institute for the year 1909 contains an article I give below which Kafka wrote as a clerk of the office. Naturally, Kafka is not mentioned by name in the report itself. But I remember exactly Kafka bringing me the annual report that year, and telling me this article was his work. His boss had corrected his draft, but Kafka's style can be seen unmistakably in passages here and there even in this technical work. The high official who was kind enough to see me also pointed out the passage, as well as another one in the annual report for 1910, and told me they were Franz Kafka's work" (pp. 82–3).

141 Ibid.

of 380 to 400 revolutions per minute. The dangers to the operator, presented by the large space between the cutter spindle and the surface of the table, are obvious."[142]

These spindles were used, Kafka explained, either because the danger was not recognized, which may incidentally have increased the danger, or with the knowledge of the presence of a permanent danger which could not be avoided.

> Although an extremely cautious operator could take care not to allow any joint of his fingers to project from the timber when guiding it over the cutter head, the main danger defied all caution. … Not only every precaution but also all protecting devices seemed to fail in the face of this danger, as they either proved to be totally inadequate or, whereas they reduced the danger on the one hand (automatic covering of the cutter slot by a protecting slide, or by reducing the width of the cutter space), they increased it on the other by not allowing the chippings sufficient space to leave the machine, which resulted in choked cutter spaces and in injured fingers when the operator attempted to clear the slot of chippings.[143]

The idea that danger that is decreased on one side and increased on another side is an aspect of the description of the postmodern understanding of risk. Here, too, Franz Kafka stands at the center of certain concerns of the contemporary world.

Presumably, Kafka believed in the utility of insurance. In general, he might have thought that it was better to have it than not to have it. The reservation that Kafka expressed is to the effect that the workers requested relief when they should demand it. "How modest these men are," Brod recalls Kafka saying. "They come to us and beg. Instead of storming the institute and smashing it to little pieces, they come to us and beg."[144] The link between insurance as, at least in the industrial insurance context, and the idea of social reform and moral obligation to one's fellows is clear.

Such linkages are evident, as noted, in the work of the philosopher Josiah Royce. At the time of the First World War, Royce published a book called *War and Insurance*, which he described as urging that "the cause of the world's peace would be aided if in the future the principle of insurance were gradually and progressively introduced into international business."[145] Royce noted that "[I]nsurance has already proved to be, in the modern life of individual nations, a cause of no little growth in social organization, in human solidarity, in reasonableness, and in peace."[146] Royce believed that the "best workings of the insurance principle have been, on the whole, its indirect workings. It has not only taught men, in manifold ways, both the

142 Ibid.

143 Ibid., pp. 83–4. Brod follows this with an outline of a working men's community that Kafka wrote at the end of his life: It was called the "Guild of Workmen Without Possessions". For Brod, at least, there seems to have been a relationship link between the impossibility of eliminating risk and the social or communitarian solution to the problem of the workers.

144 Ibid., p. 82.

145 Josiah Royce (1969), *The Basic Writings of Josiah Royce* (ed. John J. McDermott) (Chicago: Univ. of Chicago Press), p. 1135.

146 Ibid.

best means and the wisdom of "bearing one another's burdens,"[147] but it has also established many indirect, and for that very reason all the more potent, types of social linkage ..."[148]

We might also illustrate with the work of John Commons, who visited the Amana Community and rejected what he saw there, and, in response to that form of religious communitarianism, developed his own program of industrial economics, rooted, as he said, in debt rather than love.[149] In the figure of Commons, we can link labor history to utopian history, including labor organizations' and workers' industrial insurance.[150] If we can take a hint from English history, we can connect the English friendly societies (early and somewhat covert forms of unionism, we are told)[151] and fraternal organizations as insurance enterprises. These groups, often ethnic and overlapping with communitarian utopias in stressing mutual aid, are rooted in communal affiliation. They are also a piece of the story of insurance and thinking about its link to visions of the ideal society.

Thus, Metropolitan Life at one time reminds one both of a vertical company town and of a utopian community. Certainly a part of what the company was doing involved fighting off the threat of state socialism. At the same time, it is difficult to believe that the idealistic images (in language and photographs) are simply devices to sell insurance. It is more as though having insurance, which means being insurable, is a ticket to the good life. Insurance, on this reading, becomes one of the paths to

147 Galatians 6:2. (Compare 6:5 "Everyone shall bear his own burden"—both are used as mottos in Arnold Wilson and Hermann Levy (1937) *Industrial Assurance*, (London: Oxford University Press) with the suggestion that "burdens" in 6:2 means misfortune while in 6:5 it means liability.)

148 Royce, *The Basic Writings of Josiah Royce*.

149 In his autobiography, John Commons wrote: "I became suspicious of Love as the basis of social reform. I visited the Amana Community of Christian Communists in Iowa. They distinguished rigidly between love of man and love of woman. I studied Mazzini, the great Italian leader of Christian Socialism fifty years before. He founded Christian Socialism on the Duties of Man, including duties to wife and family. Eventually, after many years, in working out my institutional economics, I made Duty and Debt, instead of Liberty and Love, the foundations of institutional economics." See John R. Commons (1964[1934]), *Myself: The Autobiography of John R. Commons* (Madison, WI: University of Wisconsin Press), pp. 51–2.

150 John R. Commons (1918), *History of Labour in The United States* (New York: Macmillan).

151 See G.D.H. Cole and Raymond Postgate (1966), *The Common People* (London: Methuen University Paperbacks), p. 232.

utopia.[152] In 1887, Reverend R. Heber Newton[153] produced a list of enterprises under the heading "American Co-operation."[154] The list included fire and life insurance companies, Brook farm and Owenite and Fourierite groups, and building and loan associations.

By 1897, when the list was published as an "interesting table" in the Bliss *Encyclopedia of Social Reform*, the writer of the article on cooperation was able to say, first, that some of the enterprises on the list had failed, and, second, that the list had been broken down in the encyclopedia. Utopias were discussed under the heading "Utopias" and insurance companies were discussed under the heading "Insurance".[155] This division remains standard.

At the moment, the history of insurance is often told with an emphasis on its connections to commercial activity, to risk and to the actuarial approaches that have made risk more ascertainable and controllable. The theme of risk and the management of risk identified with modernity can be seen as central to twentieth-century life. Thus, we see a reference to "the popular contemporary theme that late modernity is characterized by the rise of the risk or insurance principle."[156]

But insurance is only a characteristic of a part of our culture. To the extent that we are concerned with a universal protection for individuals—whether or not it covers every risk—people have at times looked at state solutions. Rubinow, as the motto to the chapter indicates, thought insurance preferable to charity. It was not preferable to universally applicable state solutions. This is the subject of Chapter 4.

---

152 See Richard Russo (1998), *The Risk Pool. The Risk Pool* (New York: Vintage) (called to my attention by Tom Baker) could be presented as a novel which describes the progress of a man who is a danger to himself and others ("People who hang around your father often require hospitalization," p. 33 who is "mired in the lowest depths of the risk pool," p. 23 and then, just before his death, is classified "eligible for insurance outside the risk pool," p. 470.

153 Rev. Newton (Protestant Episcopal) was the Rector of All Souls' Church in New York. His entry in the *Dictionary of American Biography* (1928–1958) (New York: Scribner's Sons) under the auspices of the American Council of Learned Societies notes the range of his interests.

154 See R. Heber Newton (1887), *Social Studies*. (New York, London: P. Putnam's Sons), p. 86.

155 See William Bliss (ed.) (1970[1897]), *The New Encyclopedia of Social Reform*. (Westport, CT: Greenwood Press), p. 366.

156 Alan Hunt and Gary Wickham (1994), *Foucault and Law* (London: Foucault Press) p. 66.

Chapter 4

Security through the State

> Absence of fear as to the simple necessities of life, a sense of security that one belongs and, therefore, has a claim—without these what is the value of our much-vaunted civilization?
>
> I M. Rubinow[1]

This chapter directly addresses the role of government in the creation of institutions for security. There is here, as in many discussions, a focus on national activity and so the chapter includes some description of the institutions that came into existence through and after the New Deal. But there is also an attempt to say that before the New Deal there was a certain amount of activity at the state and local levels directed to the goal of individual security. Further, the chapter notes that since the institutions of private charity are also affected by government, their activities can also be understood in relation to the state.

We were told in a 1990 study that only 23 per cent of the American population believed that it was the responsibility of government to take care of very poor people.[2] In some other countries, significantly more people agreed with the statement. But as with many public opinion polls, we are left with questions here. In the question itself, no distinctions are raised relating to the cause of the poverty. Is the question understood to concern urban minorities? Widows and orphans? Men who have lost their jobs? Men disabled in accidents? And here are two additional questions: When the word responsibility is used, what does it mean? Legal responsibility? Constitutional responsibility? How would respondents have declared themselves on the proposition: "It is not the responsibility of government to take care of very poor people, but they should do so anyway." Is it possible that in this instance, as in the case of education, the absence of a constitutional directive does not quite square with the expectation of the public that education is somehow the job of government? And as to government, a different question arises. When we use this language in the United States, we immediately are involved in discussions of federalism. "Government" may mean the federal government or it may mean any level of government. Thus

---

1 Rubinow (1930): "Social Insurance – An Approach to a New Order" in Kirby Page (ed.) *A New Economic Order* (New York: Harcourt Brace and Co.), pp. 161-173.

2 Quoted in Seymour Lipset and Gary Marks (2001), *It didn't Happen Here: Why Socialism Failed in the United States*, (New York: W.W. Norton & Co.), pp. 288–89.

the question is raised: were the respondents in the survey declaring themselves against federal action only, leaving open the possibility of approval of state and local assistance?

If by "government" we mean "federal or national government," we say that this federal government was a government of limited powers, and that the states retained general powers, so called police powers. Government then meant a government in a federal system where other governments existed. Those governments often did act in those areas in which the federal government was assumed not to be able to act. Welfare was one of those areas. States and towns dealt with the poor through the poor laws, while the federal government acted only in certain emergency situations. (There is early precedent for federal action: Michele Landis[3] describes early experiences of disaster relief, and Theda Skocpol[4] describes mothers' pensions.) Novak's list of early town functions makes clear the range of local government activity. Novak's list of the functions of local governments is particularly interesting in that it clearly draws on material older than the Elizabethan poor laws. The references to forestalling and regrating have their antecedents in the regulation of the economies of the medieval world.[5]

The history of state and local responsibility for the poor in the United States is entirely familiar. Town relief for those with legal settlements, together with a system of "warning out," is very old. The cases through the nineteenth century are not, in general cases of individuals asserting their rights claims against towns, however, but rather of towns suing each other over the question of who was responsible for a particular pauper. But we are familiar in the United States with the unhappy institutions for the poor: the alms house, and the work house. Piven and Cloward argue that the circumstances of poor relief were so bad that individuals would take any job rather than accept town assistance. (Their general argument is that relief should be understood as a way of dealing with labor issues.[6]) Novak notes that there is a connection between morals regulation and poor relief as to young women found to be immoral.[7] But whatever this form of relief is, it is not laissez-faire. This does not mean, as Novak points out, that there is a direct line from those institutions, local

3 See Michele L. Landis (1998) *Let Me Next Time Be Tried by Fire: Disaster Relief and the Origins of the American Welfare State: 1789-1874*, 92 Nw. U. L. Rev. 967 pp. 697-1034.

4 Theda Skocpol (1992) *Protecting Soldiers and Mothers: The Political Origins of Social Policy in United States* (Cambridge: Belknap Press of Harvard University Press).

5 See Max Radin, (1931) *The Lawful Pursuit of Gain*, (New York: Arno 1976) p. 11 and p. 125, n. 17. Regrating was a condemned manipulation of the price of goods. Max Radin notes that "To buy goods in the hope that they will rise in value, indeed to buy them in order to resell them at all, forestalling and 'regrating' were for a long time deemed a particularly wicked and cruel type of fraud. In many parts of Europe, it is only recently that these things have ceased to be crimes."

6 See, Frances Fox Piven and Richard Cloward (1972) *Regulating the Poor: The Functions of Public Welfare*, (New York: Pantheon).

7 William Novak (1996), *The People's Welfare: Law and Regulation in the 19th Century America* (Chapel Hill, NC: University of North Carolina Press).

and very likely mean and punitive, to the New Deal.[8] But Novak's description of a "well regulated society" is far from the idea of every poor person for themselves that is sometimes thought to characterize the United States before FDR[9].

Insecurity involves often the fear of poverty, and it is possible to focus on the poor, or impoverished, or the recipients of welfare as the people involved in a consideration of state policies on security. And/or we can look at the ways in which, from time to time, government (federal or state) gave assistance to other people—those whose property was destroyed in floods for example, soldiers or mothers, and see that we are not dealing with a fixed and permanent group but rather a category into which various people might fall. They may not be poor. The idea that insecurity is largely a problem for the poor is reinforced by a contrast to the way in which we often talk about insurance, since we tend to say that insurance is not a defense against destitution but a way of using someone else's money rather than one's own to protect a style of middle-class living. That is, insurance is one of the strategies available to people who have options and who now want to reduce the amount of money that they must pay directly out of their pockets. In many instances, they do have that money. But there is insecurity here, too. First, some in the middle class may fear dropping into a lower class if their insurance claims are denied (the policy covers this sort of damage but not that). In the United States today, as noted in Chapter 3, a group particularly concerned about falling into poverty is a group of middle-class people, the very old, who fear outliving their money.

In the early part of the twentieth century, the international discussion of the best way for government (any government, but often national government) to deal with the welfare of its citizens was much debated. Large revolutionary movements provided examples of systems that were available to be tried or rejected. In 1930, *A New Economic Order* reviewed a number of these systems: capitalism, communism, socialism and fascism. The writers included some whose names are remembered (Norman Thomas, Edward Seligman) and others less well known. Part 2 of the book carried the sub-head "Ways of transforming the present competitive system into a cooperative order." It is in that part of the book that Rubinow's essay "Social Insurance" was published, along with pieces by Paul H. Douglas, A.J. Muste and Reinhold Neibuhr. These essays were directed to the question that Rubinow raised and that is used as an epigram to this chapter. What after all were the responsibilities of the government of a state and what were the various mechanisms available for insuring the welfare of the citizens of a state?

---

8 William Novak, id.

9 Roosevelt, the 32nd president of the United States, is associated with efforts to get America out of the Depression of the 1930s and with the reform programs known as the New Deal. He has remained a major point of reference for discussions of the American welfare state.

The Background Legal Regime

As noted, we often use the word "government" as though it meant federal government. We tell the story of the growth of government activity in welfare through this understanding. But there are other ideas that might be relevant to our history. For example, we can obviously consider the role of state and local government in assistance programs, workman's compensation, mothers' pensions and even education. Then we can consider the ideas that the legal system, also part of "government," offered through law. These may go together, for the law of torts and employers' liability is part of the history of workman's compensation, and often discussed. Rubinow, for example, spends time discussing the limitations of the tort law and the various defenses that made recovery for those injured in industrial accidents so uncertain.[10] But certain ideas about security and welfare also can be found in the law of contracts, and that connection is less often made.

We can provide some insight on the family and the town as a background sources of individual support by considering a nineteenth-century contracts case. *Mills v. Wyman*,[11] rests on the ordinary rules for adults who are not under the authority of their parents and are not adjudicated paupers. Briefly, they are supposed to take care of themselves. Where they cannot, and others take care of them, those others do as samaritans. This is true unless there is an enforceable promise by someone to pick up the expenses of care. The 1825 litigation in *Mills v. Wyman* concerned the enforceability of such a promise made by a man's father, and juxtaposes the interplay of family responsibility, the poor laws and the law of contracts.

A good samaritan sued a father to recover a compensation for the board, nursing, and so on, of Levi Wyman, his son. The son it was said "at the time when the services were rendered," was about 25 years of age, and had long ceased to be a member of his father's family. After all the aid had been given and the expenses had been incurred, Levi Wyman's father wrote a letter to the plaintiff, promising to pay him such expenses. The question was whether this promise could be enforced. There was no consideration for this promise, except what grew out of the relation that subsisted between Levi Wyman and the defendant father.

Parker C.J. began by noting that "general rules of law established for the protection and security of honest and fair-minded men, who may inconsiderately make promises without any equivalent, will sometimes screen men of a different character from engagements that they are bound in *foro conscientiae* to perform." This protection of some, which results in inquiry to others, is "evident in the rule that a mere verbal promise, without any consideration, cannot be enforced by action. The rule is the rule even when a refusal to perform such a promise may be disgraceful."

Here, the court continued, there was no consideration. "The kindness and services towards the sick son of the defendant were not bestowed at his request. The son was

---

10 I.M. Rubinow (1913) *Social Insurance* (New York: Henry Holt) Chapter VI, pp. 86–99.

11 *Mills v. Wyman* (20 Mass. 207 (1825)).

in no respect under the care of the defendant. He was twenty-five years old, and had long left his father's family."

The court rejected the argument that a moral obligation might support the promise. This rule assumed a pre-existing obligation, which has become inoperative by positive law. The court illustrates with moral obligations of support in the family:

> Is there not a moral obligation upon every son who has become affluent by means of the education and advantages bestowed upon him by his father, to relieve that father from pecuniary embarrassment, to promote his comfort and happiness, and even to share with him his riches, if thereby he will be made happy? And yet such a son may, with impunity, leave such a father in any degree of penury above that which will expose the community in which he dwells, to the danger of being obliged to preserve him from absolute want.

In short, the legal support obligation between son (adult) and father is only enough to keep the father off some sort of charity.

> Is not a wealthy father under strong moral obligation to advance the interest of an obedient, well disposed son, to furnish him with the means of acquiring and maintaining a becoming rank in life, to rescue him from the horrors of debt incurred by misfortune? Yet the law will uphold him in any degree of parsimony, short of that which would reduce his son to the necessity of seeking public charity.

The court's conclusion is that "[T]here are great interests of society that justify withholding the coercive arm of the law from these duties of imperfect obligation, as they are called; imperfect, not because they are less binding upon the conscience than those that are called perfect, but because the wisdom of the social law does not impose sanctions upon them." The good samaritan loses.

The description of the possible impact of the family responsibility laws is discussed.

> It has been attempted to show a legal obligation on the part of the defendant by virtue of our statute, which compels lineal kindred in the ascending or descending line to support such of their poor relations as are likely to become chargeable to the town where they have their settlement.

But this argument is rejected.

> It is a sufficient answer to this position that such legal obligation does not exist except in the very cases provided for in the statute and never until the party charged has been adjudged to be of sufficient ability thereto. We do not know from the report any of the facts which are necessary to create such an obligation. Whether the deceased had a legal settlement in this commonwealth at the time of his death, whether he was likely to become chargeable had he lived, whether the defendant was of sufficient ability, are essential facts to be adjudicated by the court to which is given jurisdiction on this subject. The legal liability does not arise until these facts have all been ascertained by judgment, after hearing the party intended to be charged.

The reference to settlement involves the principle of the old poor laws. Levi Wyman was not an adjudicated pauper and his father had not been declared responsible for him.

Even the relative responsibility laws, which attempted to enforce family obligation through law, defined the responsibility, the range of relatives responsible, in different ways, in different times and places, suggesting the changing shape of the family. We, today, operating within a middle-class idea of the nuclear family, may be startled at certain assumptions of the relative responsibility laws.[12] As to changes in family structure, we might use a distinction between family and kin. The family has grown smaller and tighter and the kin group much less significant.

Further, the idea of family care, while apparently built on some ideas of nurturing and maternalism, tends to forget the idea of the "poor relation," a person of whom traditionally much no one has much good to say (see Charles Lamb, for example).[13] When the poor relation not only takes up a place at the table but also competes with one's children for resources, it is not clear that the poor relation gets much. This may be true even in the form in which it is most common, the issue raised by the "sandwich generation" faced with responsibilities to both older and younger generations. The immigrants took care of each other, it is sometimes said. In the old days, the larger extended family provided an economic buffer and was sometimes the employer of last resort. But at a fairly large emotional cost. The poor relation was not a valued player. His—and sometimes more particularly her—very existence may have been resented. When the family business had to accommodate the incompetent son, there might be considerable tension. The idea of parasitism—the image of the welfare Queen is the one we sometimes use – runs as deep in the private sphere as in the public.

The New Deal

The New Deal itself could be framed by President Franklin Pierce and his 1854 veto of the bill that would involve the federal government in care of the indigent insane and Roosevelt's Second Bill of Rights. On vetoing the bill, Pierce noted:

> I cannot find any authority in the Constitution for making the Federal Government the great almoner of public charity throughout the United States. To do so would, in my judgment, be contrary to the letter and spirit of the Constitution and subversive of the whole theory upon which the Union of these states is founded.

Further, even:

---

12 Jacobus Ten Broek (1964), "California's Dual System of Family Law", 16 *Stanford Law Review*, 257–291.

13 Charles Lamb (1987) "Poor Relations" in *Essays of Elia and Last Essays of Elia*, (Oxford: Oxford University Press), ed. Jonathan Bate, pp. 178–187.

if it were admissible to contemplate the exercise of this power, for any object whatever, I cannot avoid the belief that it would, in the end, be prejudicial rather than beneficial to the noble offices of charity, to have the charge of them transferred from the States to the Federal Government.[14]

Another version of this story was offered by Franklin Roosevelt himself. In 1944, as part of his presentation of a Second Bill of Rights, he said: "This Republic had its beginning and grew to its present strength, under the protection of certain inalienable political rights" which were rights to life and liberty and as the nation grew, it became clear that "these political rights proved inadequate to assure equality in the pursuit of happiness." Finally, Roosevelt said, "We have come to a clear realization of the fact that true individual freedom cannot exist without economic security and independence." He quoted the language of an old English case: "'Necessitous men are not free men.' People who are hungry and out of a job are the stuff of which dictatorships are made."[15]

Quite correctly, Roosevelt's message is included in a book on human rights, [16] a field that has come to see the ideas of social security and industrial insurance in terms of fundamental rights. And certainly the emphasis on the issues of large scale risks is global.[17]

New Deal is widely represented as a serious start of welfare state in America. We are, as a country, positive about social security, seeing it as a great link between people, a form of community. David Moss, in *When All Else Fails*, sees this history as a progressively increasingly intervention, until one has, with the 1960s, *Security*

---

14 Franklin Pierce, Message to Congress 1854. Michele Landis (1998), "Let me next time be tried by fire: Disaster Relief and the Origins of the American Welfare State: 1789–1874", 92 Nw. U.L. Rev. 967 (1998) pp. 697–1034 has complicated this story by documenting the federal support of some individuals in a fairly early period. The response to catastrophes, she argued, provides the background of the federal New Deal. See also Theda Skocpol (1992) *Protecting Soldiers and Mothers: The Political Origins of Social Policy in United States* (Cambridge: Belknap Press of Harvard University Press).

It is likely that any serious history of the twenty-first century status of federal disaster relief will have to deal with the events in the Gulf States of early September 2005, centering on the failures in New Orleans, which, at the very least, reopened the question of level of governmental responsibility.

15 Franklin D. Roosevelt (1944), *State of the Union Message*, 90–1, Cong. Rec. 55, 57 (quoting *Vernon v. Bethell* (2 Eden 110, 113 1762).

16 See Frank Newman and David Weissbrot (1990), *International Human Rights* (Cincinnati: Anderson Publishing Company) p. 362.

17 See Ulrich Beck, (1986) *Risk Society: Towards a New Modernity*, (London/Newbury Park, California: Sage Publications) p. 47. Beck notes certain threats in a "risk" society, uninsurable threats, beyond risk, and in fact defined by their uninsurability by private insurance companies.

for All. [18] We continue to talk as though the New Deal provided security for those who needed it most, though this was an over-statement even at the time.

Possibly the outstanding contribution of the New Deal was the Social Security Act, or set of acts. Of these, as Linda Gordon points out, the first two are conventionally classified today as "social insurance," while the others are classified as "welfare." The consequences of the classification are clear. The people on "welfare" are stigmatized, get less money and are in a generally different and even deliberately unsympathetic structure.

To our generation, the importance of race in welfare is obvious. Recent scholarship argues that there was discrimination against blacks throughout the New Deal and, later, in such programs as the G.I. bill,[19] as the federal government accommodated itself and its services to the norms of southern segregation.[20] And as to health care, the late Charles Black wrote that "it is no great breech of probability to guess that the failure of the United States now to go to a civilized system of general medical care results, at least in part, from a reluctance to give that much to poor black people."[21]

Critics of the New Deal opposed it on ground already familiar from the international debate over social reforms: this from G.K. Chesterton:

> And as France was the standard-bearer of citizenship in 1798, Germany is the standard-bearer of this alternative solution in 1915. It can give the individual worker everything except the power to alter the State—that is, his own status.

His summary is:

> Germany gives the individual exactly the liberty that has always been given to a slave—the liberty to think, the liberty to dream, the liberty to rage; the liberty to indulge in any intellectual hypotheses about the unalterable world and state—such as have always been free to slaves, from the stoical maxims of Epictetus to the skylarking fairy tales of Uncle Remus.

Chesterton notes that defenders of slavery tend to argue that, if history has merely a material test, the material condition of the subordinate under slavery tends to be

---

18 David Moss (2002) *When All Else Fails* (Cambridge: Harvard University Press). In an introductory historical discussion Moss uses these sub-titles: security for business, security for workers and then security for all. Pp. 4–9.

19 The G.I. Bill (1944,) provided a variety of benefits for veterans who had served in the Second World War. It had a particularly significant impact in the area of education, providing support for veterans wanting to continue their education. On the history of another group (single mothers) see Linda Gordon (1994), *Pitied but Not Entitled* (New York: Free Press).

20 Ira Katznelson (2005), *When Affirmation Action was White* (New York: Norton), p.39, on decentralization as an aid to discrimination by local officials, particularly in the South.

21 Charles Black (1997), *A New Birth of Freedom* (New York: Grosset Putnam), p. 152.

good rather than bad. He once pointed out how precisely the "model village" of a great employer reproduces the safety and seclusion of an old slave estate.[22]

Following the changes of the 1960s, the problem that the New Deal had seen as aid to dependent children, became aid for families with dependent children. More recently, further changes were instituted, and a book describing American laws and legal institutions[23] could summarize the American welfare program in this way (significantly, this is part of a section on the family):

> When child support and the resources of the custodial parent are not sufficient to support the child, a "safety net" of welfare programs is available. From 1935 until 1966, the federal government funded and supervised a cooperative state-federal program that provided cash and in-kind payments to needy families with children deprived of support as a result of the absence, disability or, in some cases, the unemployment of a parent, called Aid to Families with Dependent Children (AFDC). The purpose of the program was to provide a stable source of income at a subsistence level to allow the needy children involved to be cared for at home by their parent or parents. But in 1996 Congress replaced the program with one called the Family Assistance Program. Congress determined that single parents with children at home should work and that financial assistance should be temporary until they can become self-sufficient. A two-year limit was imposed on financial assistance and various work requirements were imposed. It remains to be seen what will happen to the families involved once they get to the end of their two-year periods.
>
> In addition to cash assistance, "food stamps"—coupons redeemable for food—are available to low-income households, [as is medical assistance (called "Medicaid").[24] [Also,

22 G.K. Chesterton (1987[1916]) "The Wrong Horse" (from *The Crimes of England*) in G.K. Chesterton *Collected Works*, 2nd Vol., Part II, Vol. 5, pp. 293–374, (San Francisco: Ignatius Press).

23 William Burnham (2000) *Introduction to the Law and Legal System of the United States*, (3rd edn) (St. Paul MN: West Group) p. 512.

24 Ibid. And there may also be assistance to families with children and federal programs providing for free or reduced-price hot lunches (and sometimes breakfasts) in public schools (Burnham p. 491).

An overview of the New Deal by legal historians connects it to the development of the idea of the New Property. See *American Legal History* (2005) 3rd edn, Kermit Hall Paul Finkelstein, James W. Ely, (Oxford: New York) pp. 616–617. "The New Deal ushered in the welfare state, which included the concept of Entitlement," they write. Entitlement is defined in this context as "a claim that a person has on some benefit distributed by the government." The historians note that this is "new property" because it is not identical with the conventional understanding of property. "Considered as a property concept [the new property] differs from traditional kinds of property in that the claimant ("owner") does not have legal title … instead, he or she has a claim against a benefit." The 1960s and 1970s saw litigation in which plaintiffs argued that the new property ought to be as securely protected as the old property had been. (This argument was made against the government's claim that the 'entitlements' were really discretionary government grants.) The historical summary concludes by noting that while the Supreme Court has not adopted the position that entitlements were rights – they were matters of economic regulation, the Court also had ruled in one important case that welfare benefits could not be terminated without a hearing. "Failure to conduct such a hearing was deemed

totally disabled people, including children, are entitled to support under the Supplemental Security Income program.[25]]

The American reformers at the time of the New Deal were not, in fact, trying to create new men. They were only very selectively trying to support some of the men who were already there, and already maintaining value systems understood to be American. They have been criticized for limited ambition. But Roosevelt had, in fact, a somewhat larger ambition. In 1944, Franklin D. Roosevelt's second bill of rights (quoted in part above) was fairly specific: "We have accepted, so to speak, a second Bill of Rights under which a new basis of security and prosperity can be established for all—regardless of station, race, or creed." These rights included:

> The right to a useful and remunerative job in the industries or shops or farms or mines of the nation; The right to earn enough to provide adequate food and clothing and recreation; The right of every farmer to raise and sell his products at a return which will give him and his family a decent living; The right of every businessman, large and small, to trade in an atmosphere of freedom from unfair competition and domination by monopolies at home or abroad; The right of every family to a decent home; The right to adequate medical care and the opportunity to achieve and enjoy good health; The right to adequate protection from the economic fears of old age, sickness, accident, and unemployment; The right to a good education. All of these rights spell security ...[26]

But this expanded program never became part of the national commitment.

The New Deal had little to say about blacks. (Linda Gordon has noted that there were not many in the North. The prime concern was working men and immigrants, who were not perceived as a permanent underclass.) The Southern blacks received very little by way of state relief, but this did not concern anyone significantly. (An Alabama textbook used in the twentieth century called "slavery" the first social security program.)[27] Today, a major indictment of the New Deal programs is precisely the groups omitted: those in most serious need. As Abraham Epstein said then, it

---

a violation of procedural due process as guaranteed by the fourteenth amendment." But of course a right to process is not the same as a right to benefits. Debates over the utility of a rights analysis raise related issues. Kermit Hall, Paul Finkelstein and James W. Ely (2005), *American Legal History*, 3rd edn. (Oxford: New York), pp. 616–17.

25 In the same way that the contractual base of the insurance relationship creates an emphasis on the precise definition of responsibilities under the contract, the categorical nature of American assistance programs creates an emphasis on questions of eligibility. There is then the risk that individuals will behave in a way which creates or facilitates eligibility. A major argument for reduction of welfare benefits focused on dependent children was that women would have children so that those children would receive public benefits.

26 Samuel Rosenman (ed.) (1950), *The Public Papers & Addresses of Franklin D. Roosevelt*, Vol. XIII. (New York: Harper), pp. 40–42.

27 Virginia Van Der Vees Hamilton (1977), *Alabama: A Bicentennial History* (New York: W.W. Norton & Company) p. 57.

was a program to tax the poor for the sake of the impoverished. But some of the impoverished were omitted altogether.

In thinking about the New Deal, "welfare planners and legislators might especially have paused to consider whether traditional legal concepts of property, residence, income, the makeup of the family and the responsibilities of family members" were relevant, Ten Broek wrote.[28] These were ideas originating in other contexts and properly governing other relationships, he said. It might be urged that were other ideas more appropriate for welfare programs. "If one confines himself to the planning area of the federal Social Security Act, and again narrows that to the public assistance provisions of that measure, it is clear that no such act of imaginative originality took place."[29]

For some, like Gertrude Himmelfarb, real originality would lie in an answer along the lines of a devolution from the national state through various organizations down to the family, and abolition of the centralized guarantees of the New Deal. "If the devolution of authority from the federal government to the states is desirable, why not the devolution from the states to local governments? And if to local governments, why not to private institutions—charities, churches, community?"[30] To respond to this issue it seems that we have to consider, then, political attitudes toward security in relation to other ideas about institutions and also about religion and economics.

Rubinow on the New Deal and the Role of Private Organizations

Late in his life, Rubinow wrote two pieces addressing the questions of government and private agencies in dealing with problems of poverty. One piece[31] stressed the political strength of interest groups, including social workers, in opposing government programs. He noted that insurance organizations, lawyer groups and social workers all had special interests, usually economic, which put them into a hostile posture. Insurance groups particularly, he said, were essentially identified with employers, rather than the injured workman, in considering issues of compensation for workplace injuries. And social workers opposed mothers' aid because, in effect, they were concerned that federal programs for mothers' aid would reduce the range of social work activities. As interesting as his view of the interest group questions here is Rubinow's observation on the rewriting of history evident in this area, as all others. In effect, he said, it was hard to find anyone now to admit now that some years ago they had opposed the reform legislation.[32]

---

28 Jacobus Ten Broek (1954), "The Impact of Welfare Law Upon Family Law", *Cal. L. Rev.* 42, 458–485.

29 Ibid., p. 458. See also Bruce Ackerman and Anne Alstott (1936), *The Stakeholder Society*.

30 Himmelfarb, Introduction to De Tocqueville, *Memoirs of Papuerism*, ibid.

31 Rubinow (1931), "Public and Private Interest in Social Insurance", *American Labor Legislation Review*, p. 181.

32 *American Labor Legislation Review*, id.

Do we doubt that government at some level was supposed to deal with poverty? That the Prince, for example, was supposed to protect his people from dearth? That even a regime that indicates that the poor should have gleaning rights[33] is an expression of the idea that the ordering regime has the responsibility to structure an obligation to care for the poor in this mode? Perhaps some do, and these have argued, historically and at the moment, that family and private philanthropy was supposed to deal with the problem of the poor.

But, of course, neither the family nor private philanthropy is "private" in an ultimate sense. As to the family, this has been discussed in Chapter 2. The same point can be made about private charity. The state is deeply involved in its activities, even the to point of saying, as was said at the time of the Elizabethans, that people should not give charity under some circumstances. Thus, alms to sturdy paupers were forbidden under the English statute of laborers.[34]

MacIver's writing in 1928 described the relationship between voluntary associations and particularly those devoted to care of the poor, and the state, in these terms. The present position, he said, is somewhat as follows.

> The state in most countries has assumed a general responsibility for the poor, expressed through poor law, while leaving a wide field for the world of voluntary agencies. Possibly the state might, possibly it should, take over the tasks which these have assigned to themselves ... but it is certainly erroneous in respect of other interests which have created "voluntary" associations.

He illustrates with education:

> Here, the general attitude to the state has been to insist on universal education... while at the same time it permits, even in respect of elementary education, the independent functioning of voluntary establishments.[35]

Question of private charity are currently very important in the United States since the debate over welfare invokes importantly the existence of both private charity and family support. There is much conversation already on whether the family can, in the current world, support the job assigned to it by some writers. There is much less conversation about private charity.

Rubinow was also highly critical of both the state and insurance companies in relation to issues of security. As to the state, he writes negatively of the soldiers' pensions (used now as an example of early federal activity) on the theory that these "infamous pensions" irrationally benefited some people who had no obvious entitlement. (For example, widows of veterans who married the veterans when they were old men, long after the wars for which they were being rewarded.) As to life

---

33 Joseph Singer (2000), *The Edges of the Field* (Boston, MA: Beacon Press).

34 Stefan Riesenfeld (1955), "The Formative Era of America Public Assistance Law", *California Law Review* 43, 175–233.

35 Robert MacIver, (1928) *The Modern State*, (London: Oxford University Press) p. 167.

insurance, he was as opposed as some social workers to the practice of overselling life insurance[36] (functionally burial insurance) to people who could not afford it and would have been better off buying medical care.

There is some unexpectedness in Rubinows's writing. He is simply not someone who argued for social security consistently over decades, a missionary for the cause. He was, to begin with, also a witness and historian of the struggle. He remembered that some social workers (though they might now deny it, he says, in 1930) opposed social solutions because they might reduce the influence of private charity and cede this function to the state.[37] But in addition to thinking about social security and the government, he thought about the American college, and sectarian organizations. He criticized the college degree as producing people who had spent a good deal of expensive time and received nothing of particular value.[38] And as to charity, he distinguished clearly and thoughtfully between the functions of government and private assistance.

Rubinow was of course a strong advocate of social insurance and of the large role for government in the provision of security. What role did he see for the private sectarian charity with which he was familiar? His answer was clear: the government should deal with questions that were general, and systemic. The private Jewish charities should deal with the specialized communal problems specific to Jews qua Jews.[39]

A few years before he died, Rubinow wrote a highly personal article (on the inadequacies of the American conception of college, four years of "vacation more than vocation") in which he offered some striking self-description. He was, he said, a college man, a writer of many serious books, and someone in *Who's Who in America*. But he was not a man of means and did not "run a car—not even a Ford."[40] (In the *Quest for Security* he comments that it is easier for intellectual workers than for industrial workers to admit that they are too poor to have a car.[41])

But to a reader 70 years later, certain points about Rubinow's presentation are striking. In his first book, his sense of the family is still rooted in his background. Rubinow wrote:

---

36 I.M. Rubinow (1924, 1936) *Quest for Security*, p. 467.

37 See I.M. Rubinow, "Public & Private Interests in Social Interests" *American Labor Legislation Review* XXI (1931) 181–191 at 187.

38 He and his wife had given up travel and vacations to educate their children. I.M. Rubinow (1927), "The Revolt of a Middle Aged Father", *Atlantic Monthly*, p. 595, 593–604.

39 I.M. Rubinow (1930), "What do we owe to Peter Stuyvesant?" in *Trends and Issues in Jewish Social Welfare in the United States, 1899–1952; the history of the American Jewish social welfare, seen through the proceedings and reports of the National Conference of Jewish Communal Service.* Robert Morris, Michael Freund (1966) [1st edn) (Philadelphia: Jewish Publication Society of America).

40 Rubinow, "The Revolt of a Middle Aged Father".

41 I.M. Rubinow (1934), *The Quest for Security*, p. 13.

> Another matter which has a much greater practical importance than would appear at first glance is the compensation right of brothers and sisters. Singularly enough their rights are quite universally disregarded. Only in Italy and Russia are their rights provided for, of course following those of immediate family and dependent parents. Yet it is quite usual for a younger person to contribute to the family budget, and a more direct support of younger brothers and sisters is a matter of common occurrence in the wage-worker's life. Since over one-third of the fatal accidents occur to unmarried workmen, and since parents are only entitled to compensation when their dependency is established, many minor brothers and sisters are unjustly deprived of their means of support.[42]

By 1930, he was focused on the death of the larger kinship group and the point that economic responsibility then connected only parents and children. "

> A very extensive method of meeting the old age problems still remains within the power of the family group. In fact, this is frequently put forth as the only normal ethical and socially desirable method of handling the problem of the aged, so much so that any suggestions as to broad social policy for many years were rejected by serious students on the ground that it might interfere with this more ethical method of family provision. The point of view is based upon disregard of all modern changes, not only in the biological makeup of the family, but also of the social relationships within the family group. What are these changes? To begin with, the concept of a family, at least as a unit of economic responsibility, has been considerably narrowed down practically to children only. With the dispersion of families throughout the country, even siblings retain only a very slight moral and of course no legal responsibility, a striking change from the standards which prevailed comparatively few years ago …[43]

There is little sustained discussion of divorce in Rubinow's work on security, though he did write several articles on divorce.[44] (Rubinow talks about desertion of the wage earner, but nothing like divorce, or women-initiated divorce as we now know it. Remarriage was so common that he apparently believed that nothing in the overall pattern has changed.)

Then, there is little treatment of issues of race.[45] His workingmen are largely white, it seems, though negroes do appear once at least, in a context in which their independence is described.[46] He is not, in short, dealing with the issue of the urban underclass, of the problem of the cycles of poverty in an urban minority.

Economists sometimes begin their discussions with an axiom about scarcity. The experience of many in America—and this was how Rubinow saw it—is that there is

---

42 I.M. Rubinow (1913) *Social Insurance* (New York: Henry Holt) p. 126.

43 I.M. Rubinow (1980 reprint), *The Care of the Aged: Proceedings of the Deutsch Foundation Conference, Chicago* (New York: Arno).

44 Rubinow's work on divorce includes: (1928), "Marriage Rate Increasing Despite Divorce", 29 *Current History 1928*, pp. 289–94 and (1930), "After Divorce, What?", *The New Republic*, July 16, pp. 226–8.

45 See Martin Gilens (2005), *Why Americans Hate Welfare* (Chicago: University of Chicago Press).

46 Rubinow, *Quest for Security*, p. 590.

a world of abundance in which there is nonetheless destitution. The problem is not scarcity but distribution. (This sense that the United States was a land of abundance is oddly reflected in the European response to Norman Rockwell's *Freedom from Want*.[47] They did not like it, Rockwell wrote, because the groaning board of his painting showed something more like abundance than simply freedom from want.)[48] In this world of abundance, the poor are often viewed as unworthy, shiftless, idle, drunk. And the rich and comfortable are viewed how? Are they arrogant, ambitious, and driving? Complacent and self-satisfied? Doing right and knowing themselves to be doing right? Enjoying freedom from want, and also freedom from doubt?

Today, as at the time of the New Deal, much of the writing about security focuses on policies towards public attitude towards the poor, derived from opinion polls. As in the writing on law and economics on "preferences," the opinions are taken as they stand. But as ideologies, ideas about religion and ideas about economics form an important background to the story of the New Deal. One thing that popular Calvinism and Austrian economics share is the idea that failure is attributable to the individual who fails, rich or poor. The religious ideology may turn on an incomprehensible judgment of a Divine Sovereign. The economic view turns one some idea of failure to adequately please the consumer (Von Mises) or to adapt to changing market conditions. Attitudes about the "poor" are only a piece of this story.

Some Religious Argument

The American attitude towards the poor is also often discussed as though we know at least one formative influence: Protestant theology. The liberalism of the eighteenth century rested on Arminianism, universalism, anti-trinitarianism and a strong hostility for enthusiastic religion.[49] The Arminian form of Protestantism fits comfortably with an idea of deserts. If salvation is earned at least in part by effort, and if success is evidence of salvation, then failure, evidence of divine disfavor, is also evidence of fault.[50] The elect could be identified by their success in the material world.

47 The Four Freedoms were outlined by President Franklin Delano Roosevelt in 1942. They were freedom of religion, freedom of speech, freedom from want and freedom from fear. The illustrator Norman Rockwell did a series of paintings on the themes of the Four Freedoms.

48 Norman Rockwell (1960) *Norman Rockwell: My Adventures as an Illustrator* (Garden City, New York: Doubleday & Co) p. 43.

49 Sydney Ahlstrom (ed.), *Theology in America*. (Bobbs Merrill: Indianapolis), "Introduction", p. 39.

50 The strict Calvinist position – built on the sovereignty of God and salvation regardless of human effort – does not seem to work this way. See fn. 53 below.

A summary of the attitudes that were locked together at the times of the New Deal was given by Ellis Hawley:

> The lack of political action was also due in part of wide appeal of ideological doctrines that justified the status quo and masked the gap between ideal and reality. In the language of contemporary lawyers, politicians, and scholars the giant corporations of the late nineteenth century became "individuals" and the new corporate system became the desirable end product of "rugged individualism" and "free enterprise."[51]

The advocates of the system stressed its open aspects. Competition, actual or potential, still protected the public and stimulated economic expansion; and even if social evils did exist, nothing could be done about them, at least not in the short run. Human society, like the animal kingdom, was a product of the "survival of the fittest." This description does not, however, give the theological context in which these positions undoubtedly existed for many people.

Marjorie Kornhauser, in describing what she called "moral economic individualism," considers in detail the basic propositions of the Calvinist approach in a way that makes clear the relation between wealth and evidence of election.[52] In moral economic individualism, the religious and moral basis of American feelings about money and wealth stems from the idea that every Christian had two "callings": a general one to lead a godly life, and a specific one by which each person through their vocation would serve God by serving the common good. The idea of a calling exists in many Protestant sects. However, scholars such as Max Weber, and Americans more generally, associate it with Puritanism, particularly Calvinism. According to Weber, the Calvinist doctrines of election and predestination provided the impetus to work and the "spirit" of capitalism: under these doctrines only some people were chosen for salvation, and the decision as to who would be saved was predetermined by God. Because doubting whether a person was chosen was considered to be a lack of faith, one was duty-bound to act as if one was one of the elect. This occurred through one's special calling—by working hard and accumulating wealth for the glory of God. A person could not obtain grace from their worldly acts, because that was predestined; they could, however, obtain and express to others their certainty that they were saved. Thus, wealth became a sign of grace: God created man to work, and through work, rather than leisure or idleness, man glorified God. A person could and should work as profitably as they were able because, in so doing, they did the work of God and worked for the common good.

As to wealth, itself, Kornhauser notes, it is thus bad ethically "only in so far as it is a temptation to idleness and sinful enjoyment of life, and its acquisition is bad only when it is with the purpose of later living merrily and without care. But as a performance of duty in a calling it is not only morally permissible, but actually

---

51 Ellis Hawley (1966) *The New Deal and the Problem of Monopoly* (New Jersey: Princeton University Press).

52 Marjorie Kornhauser (1994), "The Morality of Money: American Attitude Towards Wealth and the Income Tax", *Ind. Law Journal*, 70, 119–170.

enjoined." In short, "pursuit of wealth for its own sake, for consumption's sake, was wrong, whereas the "attainment of it as a fruit of labor in a calling was a sign of God's blessing." This combination of encouraging work and discouraging spending led to an accumulation of capital "through ascetic compulsion to save." Weber had noted:

> This worldly Protestant asceticism … restricted consumption, especially of luxuries. On the other hand, it had the psychological effect of freeing the acquisition of goods from the inhibitions of traditionalistic ethics. It broke the bonds of the impulse of acquisition in that it not only legalized it, but … looked upon it as directly willed by God.
>
> Thus, the combination of economic individualism and a religious sense of calling produced the accumulation, capitalist side of moral economic individualism that encouraged capitalism through its legal, political, and moral justifications of personal accumulations of wealth.

"Holy Willie's Prayer," a satiric poem by Robert Burns, builds on the antinomian implications of the doctrine of predestination. If one is saved by grace alone, and if this decision cannot be undone, then it doesn't matter how one behaves.[53] (Arminians respond to this by including in their theology a human contribution.)

The central question becomes: How may I know that I am among the elect? Max Weber answered this way: "Accumulation was not meritorious per se, but, in the religious sense, it was evidence of a special calling or grace." Success was evidence, not reward. Moreover, Weber said, "it was good from an economic sense only to the extent that it spurred economic growth and allowed the masses to improve their lives economically and morally. Excess wealth should not be spent on one's self nor amassed for one's heirs; it should be used to improve society."

A very detailed answer, from a Calvinist writer in the 1930s, included ideas of inner certainty.

> One may as well ask, How do I know that I am a loyal American citizen, or how shall I distinguish between white and black, or between sweet and bitter? Every one knows instinctively what his attitude is toward his country, and the Scriptures and conscience give as clear evidence of whether or not we are among God's people as white and black do of their color, or sweet and bitter do of their taste. Every person who is already a child of God should be fully conscious of the fact. Paul exhorted the Corinthians, "Try your own selves, whether ye are of the faith; prove your own selves," II Cor. 13:5.[54]

> In regard to spiritual matters, a state of doubt is a state of misery. The assurance that Christians can never be separated from the love of God is one of the greatest comforts of the Christian life. To deny this doctrine is to destroy the grounds for any rejoicing among the saints on earth; for what kind of rejoicing can those have who believe that they may

---

53 Burns "Holy Willie's Prayer" in *Selected Poems of Robert Burns* (ed. Carol McGuirk (Penguin: London) pp. 20–22); See also Hogg, *History of a Justified Sinner* on the doctrine and the interpretation.

54 Lorraine Boettner (1932), *The Reformed Doctrine of Predestination* (Phillipsburg, NJ: Presbyterian and Reformed Publishing), p. 310.

at any time be deceived and led astray? If our sense of security is based only on our changeable and wavering natures, we can never know the inward calm and peace which should characterize the Christian. To me such a doctrine has terrors which would cause me to shrink away from it forever, and which would fill me with constant and unspeakable perplexities.[55]

One can speculate on the influence of this orientation, from a strict Calvinist position, on other versions of Protestantism. It seems possible that it is at least a question worth investigating. Here is a reference to that certainty in Somerset Maughan's early novel, *Mrs. Craddock.* A man has "that magnificent faculty of always doing right and knowing it which is said to be the most inestimable gift of the true Christian."[56] One can also quote the *Thirty-Nine Articles*[57] on predestination and election. Consideration of election is full of "sweet pleasant and unspeakable comfort to godly persons" and those who "feel in themselves the working of the spirit of Christ."[58] Then there are others, who are "curious and carnal", lacking the spirit of Christ (the categories have to be applied, of course).

Uncertainty was viewed as something linked to Arminianism and a doctrine close to the idea of works. The true Calvinist was clear and certain. One could be reassured about one's own salvation by one's own success in the world. And the corresponding point was that there was nothing to be done about the condition of the poor.[59]

They could always change. Indeed, for as long as the West was open, it may even be that there was some rational basis for saying that work was always available.[60]

Professor Henry May wrote:

To those who had succeeded, the churches preached, or course, the excellence of charity. Often generosity, like morality and religion itself, was pronounced conducive to business success. Quite as often, however, it was proclaimed as a positive duty. The ancient Protestant doctrine of the stewardship of wealth was preached again and again, with warnings for those who neglected to use their gains in the Divine service.

But it is also true that there was a certain limit placed on charity by the "widespread belief in the unalterable depravity of the poor. Over and over religious

---

55 Lorraine Boettner, *The Reformed Doctrine of Predestination*, p. 194. Compare the view of Learned Hand, quoted in Gerald Gunther (1994), *Learned Hand*, (New York, Knopf) p. 549. "What then is the spirit of liberty? I cannot define it; I can only tell you my own faith. The spirit of liberty is the spirit which is not too sure that it is right." (This is taken from a speech delivered at a 1944 "I Am an American Day" in New York.)

56 Somerset Maugham, (1994[1990]) *Mrs. Craddock.* (New York: Penguin), p. 146.

57 (American revision 1801, XVII).

58 See Mark Noll, *Confessions and Catechisms of the Reformation* (Baker Publishing Group) for 1571 version.

59 The complacency seems in effect, to be generalized to something about everything being roughly as it should be.

60 Henry F. May (1949, 1967) *Protestant Churches and Industrial America* (New York: Harper Torchbooks).

writers insisted that poverty, like riches, was generally deserved. A staunch Calvinist could put this doctrine of reprobation in even more severe terms. Admitting that circumstances might have something to do with the origins of "ignorance, indolence, and immorality," the Reverend Charles Wood declared that "they soon become, exceptional cases aside, a necessary inheritance, an inborn, entailed evil, with all the force and regularity of law, transmitting their image from one generation to another, and creating conditions of life, which either discourage or crush out every ennobling aspiration …"

"For this doomed group," May wrote of the nineteenth-century position, "it was thought that not much could be done." Benevolent associations, missions, and the like generally did more harm than good except when they were authorized to remove children from their noxious environment. Pauperism and vagrancy were to be punished.[61]

May notes that "extremes of hostility to the unfortunate are not representative of the majority of Protestant opinion in the postwar period. Many church members believe heartily in the utility of working to alleviate distress." "But still the historian comes back to the idea that there were limits on the idea of serious change. "[E]ven some of the most philanthropic agreed with the *Independent* that a permanent solution to the problems of poverty was not only impossible but undesirable." He quotes in the *Independent*:

> The poor we have with us always; and this is not the greatest of our hardships, but the choicest of our blessings. If there is anything that a Christian may feel thankful for, it is the privilege of lifting a little of the load of some of his heavily-burdened neighbors.[62]

And then he refers to those who adhered to the idea later to be codified and debated as part of the "frontier theory". Here, the point was that "so long as thousands upon thousands of acres of magnificent soil can be secured beyond the Mississippi at a merely nominal price, no man who is blessed with health and willingness to work, be his family large or small, need come to the poorhouse."[63]

By the time of the Great Depression, the idea that going west would solve the problem of poverty was no longer true. And it was no longer true that private

---

61 Henry F. May (1949, 1967), *Protestant Churches and Industrial America*, (New York: Harper Torchbooks). Charles Wood, quoted in May, p. 54.

62 (1874), *Independent*, November 26, p.14. Quoted in May, p. 54. For more on the text *The Poor You Will Always Have With You*, see discussion of Wallis in Chapter 5. On some of the lessons of the Old Testament, see the letter quoted in Simon Blackburn, *Being Good: A Short Introduction to Ethics* (Oxford, Oxford University Press), 2001, 11–12. Raising such questions as "I would like to sell my daughter into slavery, as it suggests in Exodus 21:7. In this day and age, what do you think would be a fair price for her?".

63 (1870), March 17, p.4. Similarly, the *Watchman and Reflector* insisted that "In this country, every industrious, prudent, skillful, healthful laborer can acquire a handsome competence by the time he is fifty years old, if that is what he desires" *Watchman and Reflector* (1871), November 16, p. 6. Quoted in May, p. 55.

philanthropy was viewed seriously as a solution to the problems of the ill and to the aged. But the attitude toward the poor remained.[64]

It might be that the Bible taught that what was given could be taken away.[65] Weber notes that the Protestants were particularly interested in the book of Job. It described both the sovereignty of God and the favors of God, ultimately at least.[66] But the lesson was complacency for those who had been rewarded.

James Agee, describing the southern middle-class response to the situation of the white sharecroppers quotes them as saying "they are used to it."[67] Another psychological point is that we do not maintain a consistent attitude towards the poor or the impoverished, particularly to the extent that they are criminal and threatening. This failure to maintain stance is even evident in the context of the "poor relation," as Charles Lamb showed in his essay. He started by writing something comic, but somehow it turned tragic on him.[68]

Moynihan's account of the failure of the 1970's effort to achieve a guaranteed minimum wage makes a different point, which is the continuing role of a very American cultural pattern relating to moral judgments. The arguments against the proposal were less ideological than moral, it seems. People did not want to support a population that did work but spent its time making love and having babies. [69]

Some Economic Argument

In this discussion of economics, sentences from economists across centuries and from different schools are juxtaposed. The defense is that on some essential points they seem to share an orientation. Not only the "self-interest" as the primary human motivation (the central idea of Adam Smith), but also the point that the market does not protect vested interests. To the extent that economists are serious about the point that economics is a method, one would expect to find disagreements about policy conclusions, and some of these disagreements are brought to the surface here, if only to indirectly comment on those presentations that assume that only one conclusion can follow from an economic analysis of a problem. That is, the examination here is not focused on the validity of any particular proposition; rather, the point is that the propositions are different from each other.

---

64 See Michelle Landis, *Let me next time be tried by fire*, for another attempt to summarize this.

65 See Job, passim.

66 Max Weber (1930, 1997) *Protestant Ethic and the Sprit of Capitalism* (trans. Alcott Parsons) (London: Routledge).

67 Walker Evans and James Agee (1939, 1960), *Let Us Now Praise Famous Men* (Boston: Houghton Miffline).

68 Charles Lamb (1987) "Poor Relations" in *Elia and the Last Essays of Elia* ed., Jonathan Bate (Oxford: Oxford University Press) pp. 178–184.

69 Daniel Moynihan (1973) *The Politics of a Guaranteed Income* (New York: Random House) discussing debate at p. 573.

The prominence of a particularly abstract kind of economics in the law schools and the academic world generally results for some in the need for a restatement of arguments made some time ago.[70] The significance of this libertarian school, sometimes called the "Chicago School" is made more obvious by its linkages to the political world and the current demand for a smaller national presence in American life.

But in the same way that in the political world the idea that there should be a return to the pre-New Deal constitution is not a universal view, the libertarian abstractions are not the only style of economics available. While "economics," as a discipline, rests on ideas such as "rationality" and "scarcity," there are approaches that are more interested in empiricism and behavioral variation, as well as in government's role in filling in market failures, than the Chicago school would generally allow. A richer sense of the map of modern economic thinking is offered in Bernstein's *A Perilous Progress*,[71] and an even more complex view in some of the commentary on that book which includes European perspectives and especially Von Mises.[72]

The point in the present chapter is not to fully describe or argue with any of those the descriptions of "economics," but rather to say that even among those writers ordinarily classified as supporters of the free market, and hostile to state intervention, there are differences in how they approach the specific issue of poverty and welfare.

Chapter 5 of this book briefly reviews basic income and related proposals. Even here, there is not extensive argument for this particular solution, in large part because

70 Thus, Herbert Hovenkamp writing about "The first great law and economics movement," said that one of the purposes of his article on the discipline in the 1880s was to attack the notion that the present form of economic argument was the only one available. Herbert Hovenkamp (1990), "The First Great Law and Economics Movement", *Stanford Law Review* 42, 93, 933–1058.

71 "Perspectives" in the *European Journal of the History of Economic Thought*, Esther-Mirjam Sent, Roger Backhouse, A.W. Bob Coats, John B. Davis and Harold Hagemann 12: 1, 127–46.

72 A short exposition of Von Mises central ideas is found in his introduction to a book on the Incas, seen as socialist slavery. Louis Baudin (1961[1928]), *A Socialist Empire, The Incas of Peru* (trans. Katherine Woods), Van Nostrand. (Princeton, NJ: Van Nostrand) Von Mises *Foreword* pp. v–xi. The current American political argument on state intervention and the evils of liberalism sometimes locate intellectual roots in the work of Richard Epstein who sees economics as a set of simple and universal propositions. See Richard Epstein, *Simple Rules for a Complex World* (1995) (Cambridge: Harvard University Press). See also David Kirkpatrick "Seeing Slavery in Liberalism Federal Judge Janice Rogers Brown, African-American daughter of Alabama sharecroppers," *New York Times*, June 9, 2005, p. A 22. The word liberalism can be used in different ways. In the *New York Times* headline above, it refers to a particular political theory. Brian Bix notes that this usage is understood as leftist or progressive, and usually involves "support for egalitarianism, government responsibility to help the poor, resdistribution of income and like policies." Brian Bix (2004) *Dictionary of Legal Theory* (Oxford: Oxford University Press) "liberalism" pp. 128–129, at 129. Richard Epstein's position is sometimes referred to as liberatarian.

others have given a great deal of time to developing this argument and responding to the arguments of others. Thus, there is nothing here on how specifically to deal with the issue of stipends for children. As Goodin noted, any one of a number of possible solutions would seem to be an advance over what we are doing now.

Rubinow's question, used as the motto to this chapter, suggests that a serious question is one of justification. How do we justify the continuation of economic disparity, and particularly how to we justify economic inequality of the kind we see, and see growing, in the United States? It is a question put in different ways. Sometimes it is how do we justify? Sometimes it is addressed to the mind of the poor: Why don't the poor soak the rich? Ian Shapiro asked a question addressed to the elites who think about justification. Sometimes it takes the form of the questioner in Montaigne's essay: Why don't the poor burn down the houses of the rich?[73] One answer is that while the poor seem to want to rise sufficiently to live in those houses, that there are actually limits to their desire to "rise."[74]

It might be that their answer is that the rich or richer don't care or don't notice. Or that, along the lines Ian Shapiro suggests, that there are serious failures of imagination involved and that there is an empathy gap.[75] The poor cannot imagine being significantly better off. The rich cannot imagine things being so bad that they will be that poor. Or it might be that certain economic laws require poverty, and that nothing serious can be done about inequality.

The impact of economic analysis in law is so pervasive at the moment that it is difficult to find writing that does not at least gesture in the direction of that language and method. Thus, Cass Sunstein's recent book on the second Bill of Rights, stresses the point that we would have to pay attention to incentives in various directions.[76] This book, like others, is intended for a general and not a scholarly audience. The point is that the vocabulary of economics, like the vocabulary of psychology and psychoanalysis, has passed into the general culture.

And that is an accurate statement of what an economic analysis would ask us to do. The general idea is that economics is a method of analysis that forces us to think about consequences that are beyond the immediate problem that we are dealing with. It will predict consequences by projecting rational behavior from particular incentives.[77] We will distinguish, then, between immediate and long-range consequences. We will be interested in the possibility of consequences which are not

---

73 Michel de Montaigne (1989[1968]), "Of Cannibals", in *Complete Essays of Montaigne* (trans. Donald Frame), (Stanford, CA: Stanford University Press) No. 31, 150–159.

74 Michael Young (1959), *The Rise of the Meritocracy* (New York: Random House). Also: Walter Kirn (2005), "Life in the Meritocracy", *The Atlantic Monthly* 295:1, 142–154.

75 Ian Shapiro (2002) *Why the Poor Don't Soak the Rich*, 131 (Daedalus) 118–128.

76 Sunstein, (New York: Basic Books) 194–197.

77 See also Henry Hazlitt (1962, 1996) *Economics in One Lesson*, (San Francisco: Laissez Faire Books)..

intended. But as to the ultimate policies, goals and the underlying values, economists may be as divided as anyone else.[78]

And it is clear enough that even among those broadly associated with a limited or no government approach to policies, there can be differences in prescriptions. Some of these, as David Friedman has noted, are about accommodating oneself to current reality, a stance that forces compromises. Some are a result of attaching a goal to a particular condition as in Milton Friedman's support for a negative income tax, but only if it was a substitute for all other welfare programs. Others, like Hayek, seem to be supporting something which—as in Hayek's willingness to deal with poverty, but only outside the market—Van Parijs (and more pointedly Epstein)[79] suggest sits uneasily with their general views.

Economists may begin their discussions with an axiom about scarcity. Scarcity, in the sense that economists use it, is not a matter of destitution, let alone destitution in the middle of affluence. Rather, it is a technical term making the point that economic goods are not free.[80] But, as noted, the observation of many in the United States is that there is a world of abundance in which there is nonetheless destitution. The axiom and abstraction becomes true and not true. To the extent that it is felt to be somehow false, it might be thought that an imperative was created to at least deal with the problem by complicating the description. But economics as a discipline also brackets certain kinds of substantive questions. Economic analysis also does not, for example, deal with the mechanisms involved in the creation of preferences. Thus, to illustrate, a study of the consequences of income maintenance done in 1986, determined (inter alia) that people worked less and divorced more. But there was no inquiry into the question whether the divorces were in specific cases good or bad, or whether working less might in some instances be a good, as for example, when it frees up the worker or others to engage in non-work behaviour.[81] But it is not hard to

78 George Stigler (1972) "The Law and Economics of Public Policy: A Plea to the Scholars" (1) *Journal of Legal Studies*, 1–12.

79 Richard Epstein, "Hayekian Socialism", *Maryland Law Review* (1989) pp. 271-297. See also discussion in E. Phelps, (1997) *Rewarding Work: How to Restore Participation and Self Suport to Free Enterprise* (Cambridge: Harvard University Press), pp. 137–138.

80 Samuelson and Nordhaus offer a definition in the glossary of *Economics*: "Scarcity is the distinguishing characteristic of an economic good. That an economic good is scarce does not mean that it is rare, but only that it is not freely available for the taking. To obtain such a good one must either produce it or offer other economic goods in exchange." Paul A. Samuelson and William D. Nordhaus (1995), *Economics*, 15th edition. (New York: McGraw Hill).

81 "Demand" is also a term of art, having nothing to do with need. See Joan Robinson (1947), *Introduction to the Theory and Employment* (London: Macmillan). "Demand" implies money expenditure not desire or need" (p. 2). See William Forbath on general issues of work "non-work" and basic income "Symposium: The Constitution and the Experiment" and "The Obligation of Government to Secure the Material Conditions for a Good Society: Constitutional Welfare Rights: A History, Critique and Re-construction", *Fordham Law Review* 69, (2001) 1821–1891.

imagine that the results of this study will be used, as its findings resulted in the policy conclusion that income maintenance is to be avoided.

We can illustrate economic analysis further with Arthur Leff's story of the poor widow evicted by the landlord, a version of the Antillico Kirksey story. "There is this ole widow, see, with six children," Leff wrote. "It is December and the weather is rotten." She defaults on the mortgage on her (and her babies') family home. The mortgagee, twirling his black moustache, takes the requisite legal steps to foreclose the mortgage and throw them all into the cold. She pleads her total poverty to the judge. Rising behind the bench, the judge points her and her brood into the swirling blizzard. "Go," he says. "Your plight moves me not." "How awful," you say?

"Nonsense," says the economic analyst:

> If the old lady and kids slip out into the storm, they most likely won't die. There are people a large part of whose satisfactions come from relieving the distress of others, who have, that is, high utilities for beneficence and gratitude. So the costs to the widow are unlikely to be infinite. Moreover, look at the other side of the (you should pardon the expression) coin. What would happen if the judge let the old lady stay on just because she was out of money? First of all, lenders would in the future be loathe to lend to old widows with children. I don't say that they wouldn't lend at all; they'd just be more careful about marginal cases, and raise the price.[82]

It is not so strange to say everyone might at some point or other be poor, particularly if we think that the idea is relative and might mean different things to different people. "Holmes was like all Yankees," a New Dealer commented. "He was a capitalist. I will always remember what a friend said: 'One of my contemporaries lost his capital. He might as well be dead.'"[83]

Free market thinking opposes vested interests. Writers want to protect the market, but not individuals who do well in some particular moment in the market. They too are asked to take risks. But we might not acknowledge that risks means different things to different people. The rules of argument indicate that *ad hominem* approaches should be avoided, and that it is ideas that count. The speaker's personal identity, while it might have some relevance somewhere, does not in general absolutely disqualify, though certain comments are sometimes in order, whether we are talking about race, religion or class. At the same time, narratives of personal experience—they may be denigrated as anecdotal rather than significantly statistical—do show up even in formal discussions that are not in the sub-genre of narrative writing. Richard Epstein told us what his father, a radiologist taught him; and a reviewer of Epstein's book (a defense of the free market and a rejection of government health care programs) responded by describing what *his* father, a man who lost his pension twice, taught

82 Arthur Leff (1974), "Economic Analysis of Law: Some Realism about Nominalism", *Virginia Law Review* 60, 451–482, 460 ff.

83 Thomas Corcoran quoted in Katie Louchheim (1984) (ed.), *The Making of the New Deal: The Insiders Speak* (Cambridge: Harvard University Press), p. 23.

him.[84] We read with one eye on the author. We ask: Where is he or she coming from? One can "come from" many places and many of them are not directly experiential. We are taught a great deal, from teachers, from books. We absorb a great deal from the air of our culture. And out of all this we have greater or lesser empathy for the experience of others. For some, to be "constantly at risk" means something about the risks they take in their writing from a tenured platform. For others, it means something more basic to life. And there is everything in between.

There is a notable difference here between libertarian and, for example, canonist thinking that come into play here. Ambrose, in the fourth century, followed by Aquinas, followed by Canon Law, wanted to protect people in their station in life.[85] Some of our existing law may be focused the same way. But the serious libertarian agenda is quite different. And some of those who in general oppose government intervention are flexible on the point of government aid in certain contexts. Hayek was willing to have government work outside the market to take care of those who couldn't work. Hayek was open to some form of minimum income:

> There is no reason why in a free society government should not assure to all a protection against severe deprivation in the form of an assured minimum income, or floor below which nobody need descend. To enter into such an insurance against extreme misfortune may well be in the interest of all; it may be felt to be a clear moral duty of all to assist, within the organized community, those who cannot help themselves.[86]

Von Mises, less so, it seems. Von Mises noted that the concept of security as held by the wage earner was analogous to the idea held by capitalists:

> In the same way in which capitalists want to enjoy permanently an income which is not subject to the vicissitudes of changing human conditions, wage earned and small farmers want to make their revenues independent of the market. The idea is that no further occurrence should impair their own position ...
>
> But a characteristic feature of the unhampered market society is that it is no respecter of vested interests. Past achievements do not count if they are obstacles to further improvement.

Von Mises takes a hard line here:

---

84 Thomas Greaney (1998), 96 *Michigan Law Review*, 1825, at 1851 "How many libertarians does it take to fix the health care system?" (review of Epstein, *Mortal Peril*).

85 See Brian Tierney (1998), *Medieval Poor Law*. (Berkeley, CA: University of California Press), pp. 1825–1851. The doctrine of necessaries as we find it in contracts and family law (permitting a wife or child to pledge the credit of the husband/father to obtain necessaries) is unusually explicit about class in that it defines necessaries in terms of 'station in life'.

86 Chiaki Nishyama and Kurt R. Leube, *The Essence of Hayek* [Friedrich Hayek] (Stanford, California: Hoover Institution Press) p. 87. His concern was that this assistance, to provide for that person, "who, for any reason, was unable to earn in the market an adequate maintenance" should be "outside the market."

it is certainly true that the necessary of adjusting oneself again and again to changing conditions is onerous. But change is the essence of life.[87]

By contrast, Milton Friedman was a proponent of a negative income tax and opposed Moynihan's guaranteed minimum, very much like it, because it did not substitute for other welfare programs but was added to it. Not a pure enough reform in effect:

> The negative income tax would be a satisfactory reform of our present welfare system only if it replaces the host of other specific programs that we now have. It would do more harm than good if it simply became another rag in the ragbag of welfare programs.[88]

Some descriptions are so lacking in empathy that we wonder what the air is that the writer breathes or what really the background is. Did Marie Antoinette really say: "Let them eat cake?" Perhaps not. But the language has stood since the French Revolution as the ultimate example of the person without empathy and therefore without understanding.

Writing on poverty at times has some of this quality. It raises the question whether the writer is one with the strength to bear the misfortunes of others. This quality was evident even to a defender of the economic approach. Henry Hazlitt wrote:

> we ought not to concentrate only on its long-run results to the community as a whole. This is the error often made by the classical economists. It resulted in a certain callousness toward the fate of groups that were immediately hurt by policies or developments which proved to be beneficial on net balance and in the long.[89]

One striking point is the range of opinion on the question of public assistance even from those who are in general opposed to government interventions. DeToqueville's essay on poverty is fundamentally addressed to government support of the able-bodied worker. It does not doubt the need for public support of the aged, infirm, or insane. Henry Hazlitt takes no position at all on whether there ought to be government interventions on behalf of displaced workers, simply identifying certain possibilities. (Hazlitt's general position is that economics is a method that stresses long-term consequences where most people see only short-term consequences.)

One story about heaven is that heaven is a place where people pray all day and hell a place where people are perpetually in torment. I have been told that there is a Jewish version of this story that says that in fact there is really only one place, where people pray and study all day and for some people that is heaven and for other people hell. It is a story that pointedly reminds us that people have very different ideas about the kind of society—and also heaven—that they want. In part for this

87 Ludwig Von Mises (1947, 1963 rev. edn) *Human Action: A Treatise on Economics*, (San Francisco: Fox & Wilkes) pp. 852–3.

88 Milton Friedman and Rose Friedman (1980) *Free to Choose: A Personal Statement*, (New York, Harcourt) p. 122.

89 Henry Hazlitt (2962, 1996), *Economics in One Lesson* (San Francisco, Laissex Faire Books) p. 5.

reason, federalism has commended itself to many people.[90] But some coherence is necessary. At the level of social policy on security, we ought to have some idea of what it is we are trying to achieve.

To the extent that we look to the state for solutions to the systemic issues involved here, we are up against some old truths. According to one view, the seriously important questions in life are never answered finally, but only provisionally. Certainly it seems that questions about the organization of economic life have been constant, and the terms of the debate constant, for a long time. Keynes's 1926 description of the two points of view represented the debate of his time in England, of the New Deal in the United States, and it also characterizes much of the contemporary discussion.[91] Keynes wrote:

> The truth is that we stand mid-way between two theories of economic society. The one theory maintains that wages should be fixed by reference to what is "fair" and "reasonable" as between classes. The other theory—the theory of the economic Juggernaut—is that wages should be settled by economic pressure, otherwise called "hard facts," and that our vast machine should crash along, with regard only to its equilibrium as a whole, and without attention to the chance consequences of the journey to individual groups.[92]

It is striking that Bruce Ackerman and Anne Alstott, addressing hypothetical questioners in *The Stakeholder Society*, identify those people as liberals and libertarians. Recently, perhaps for the first time since the Goldwater campaign, serious free market no-government arguments have entered the mainstream debate. For those interested in law and economics, the ideas of the Austrian Economists or Milton Friedman or Richard Epstein, are central.[93]

In our constitutional debates, we associate the idea that the federal government should do very little with a supreme court that struck down progressive legislation. We cite *Lochner v. New York* (198 US 45 1905). We are accustomed to quote the line of Oliver Wendell Holmes dissenting that the constitution does not enact Herbert Spencer's *Social Statics*.[94] But perhaps we no longer have clearly in mind what Herbert Spencer thought.[95] In *Social Statics*[96] (1851), Herbert Spencer wrote:

---

90 Federalism and then pluralism.

91 John Maynard Keynes, *Essays in Persuasion* (New York: W.W. Norton & Co).

92 John Maynard Keynes, *Essays in Persuasion*, pp. 261–62.

93 Jeffrey Rosen, (2005), "The Unregulated Offensive", *New York Times Magazine*, April, 17, Section 6, p. 42, Col. 1.

94 *Lochner v New York* 98 US 45 (1905) dissent.

95 Crane Brinton asked "who now reads Spencer?" Crane Brinton (1933), *English Political Thought in the Nineteenth Century* (London: Bouverie House, Ernest Benn), p. 226. But in America, we have at least kept the name of Spencer alive, through the famous sentence of Oliver Wendell Holmes.

96 Herbert Spencer, *Social Statics* (1851, 1969) (New York: Augustus Kelley Publishers).

> It seems hard that widows and orphans should be left to struggle for life or death. Nevertheless, when regarded not separately, but in connection with the interests of universal humanity, these harsh fatalities are seen to be full beneficence—the same beneficence that brings to early graves the children of diseased parents … Under the natural order of things society is constantly excreting its unhealthy, imbecile, slow vacillating, faithless members. If they are sufficiently complete to live, they do live, and it is well that they should live. If they are not sufficiently complete to live, they die, and it is best they should die.[97]

Spencer believed that acquired characteristics were inherited. The best were passing on their various excellences at the same time that the weaker were dying off.

> Unthinking, though well-meaning, men advocate an interference which not only stops the purifying process, but even increases the vitiation—absolutely encourages the multiplication of the reckless and incompetent by offering them an unfailing provision, and discourages the multiplication of the competent and provident by heightening the prospective difficulty of maintaining a family.[98]

It would seem that:

> … [t]hese considerations seem conclusive against all relief to the poor—voluntary as well as compulsory. … But there is no objection to "helping men to help themselves," thus private charity was perhaps a good effort. Accidents will still supply victims on whom generosity may be legitimately expanded. Men thrown upon their backs by unforeseen events, men who have failed for want of knowledge inaccessible to them, men ruined by the dishonesty of others, and men in whom hope long delayed has made the heart sick, may, with advantage to all parties, be assisted.[99]

But, often, charity was seen to be wasted. Andrew Carnegie (an admirer of Herbert Spencer) said: "Of every thousand dollars spent in so-called charity nine hundred and fifty of them had better be thrown into the sea …"[100]

Commenting on the language of Oliver Wendell Holmes on Herbert Spencer,[101] Judge Richard Posner suggests that the language of Holmes about Spencer's Social Statics is one of the "great sentences in law," a "form of literary expression, making a book stand for a whole system of thought."[102] And this may well be why we no longer read Spencer. We think we know more or less what his school of thought says. The danger is that our sense of this school may be over generalized. We may miss

97 Spencer, "Poor Laws", pp.322–326. The language on the complete surviving is from the essay on *Sanitary Supervision: Social Statics* (pp. 372–395, quotation at p. 380).

98 Spencer, "Poor Laws", p. 324.

99 Spencer, "Poor Laws", p. 325–26.

100 A. Vandyke (ed) (1920) *Autobiography of Andrew Carnegie* (New York: Houghton Mifflin).

101 Holmes from Lochner, *Lochner v New York*, 98 US 45 (1905).

102 Richard Posner (1993) *Stanford Law Review* 1671 "Symposium on Civic and Legal Education: Panel Two: Legal Scholarship and Disciplinary Politics: Discussion". Posner's comments are at 1679–1683.

that Adam Smith, for example, taken as the representative of the tradition in which self-interest is dominant as a motivator of action, was surprisingly sympathetic to the poor and favored high wages for workers on the grounds of equity, as Gertrude Himmelfarb suggests in *The Idea of Poverty*. And we may miss that Adam Smith referred to the "vile maxim" of the masters of the world: "All for our selves and nothing for other people."[103] We may miss that Hayek, for example, was at least open to assistance (outside the market) for those who needed it. And seeing the brutality of Spencer's social Darwinism, we may miss the extraordinary sense of future possibility that it might contain.[104] Fiske conceived of a blend of Darwinism and Christianity, writing that "the future is lighted for us with the radiant colours of hope. Strife and sorrow shall disappear. Peace and love shall reign supreme ..."[105] Can we retain some part of the vision without the ferocity and without the sectarianism? Some approaches to these questions are suggested in Chapter 5.

---

103 Adam Smith, (1904 [1976]) *The Wealth of Nations* (Chicago: University of Chicago Press) p. 437.

104 John Fiske (1884), *The Destiny of Man* (Boston, MA: Houghton Mifflin), pp. 118–19.

105 Ibid.

Chapter 5
Security and Individualism

As against the comparatively simple solution of the problem through the patriarchal family of the agricultural past, against the beautiful and perfect solution through organized and cooperative social effort of the Utopian future, there stands out to-day the very realistic problem of the individualistic present.

I.M. Rubinow[1]

Here is a summary of the argument to this point.

Security for individuals rests on three pillars or as is sometimes said three legs of a stool. These are variously described, and sometimes there are more than three. But staying with three, we have, for example, this: "… A popular metaphor to describe the income sources for retirement is the three legged stool with social security being just one of the legs. The other two are private savings (which includes home equity) and benefits from employer sponsored retirement plans."[2]

The basic three are described in the present work as: family, insurance, government. Others have focused on the strengths of these institutions. The argument here is that each of these three pillars has weaknesses. The weakness of the family in providing security is that it is too small, too susceptible to dissolution and reshaping, and in American society, too committed to a sense of obligation based on affection to guarantee long-term security. Private insurance has weaknesses. As an institution based on contract, it will move to stricter interpretations of a contract if times are bad and permit more latitudes if times are easier. Moreover, the idea of risk classification tends to mean that the more people that need insurance, the more expensive it will be and in some cases it won't be available at all. In general, insurance tends to preserve the middle class in its position, and even here there are substantial risks that insurance does not cover. And as to the state—referred to here as government to emphasize its historically contingent aspect—governments are highly variable about their commitments to security. Policies change. This may be particularly true in the United States, where some policies are put into place as experiments whose results will be evaluated when known.[3]

---

1 I.M. Rubinow (1934) *The Quest for Security* (New York: Henry Holt), p. 226.

2 William J. Turner (2005), *Materials on Family Wealth Management*. (St Paul, MN: Thomson/West), p. 565.

3 See Teitelbaum's idea of the natural experiments in family law. Lee Teitelbaum and Laura Dupaix (1988), "Alternative Dispute Resolution and Divorce: Natural Experimentation

Two of the three pillars are sometimes seen as relatively free of government (family and market) One, of course, is itself government. Each pillar assumes the existence and functioning of the other.

One approach, following the "summary-of-the-argument-thus-far," would take us to normative questions relating to each of the three pillars. What definition of family, in the midst of the current debate over definitions on the family, would serve security best? What things should insurance companies do or do better? More rational relationship between criteria for rates and the rates themselves? More moves in the direction of universal coverage? No redlining? No use of genetic information? And as to the state, such a discussion would review the various welfare schemes in place in the United States and urge some and reject others.

A defect in this approach is that it minimizes the most general issues relating to the state activity that supports all three pillars, a point made repeatedly in this book. The hand of government and law is behind much "voluntary" or "private" action and behind ideas of property, and marriage for example. Moreover, this approach would keep our attention focused largely on what is immediately possible. It is a kind of concession to the "normative power of the actual"[4] in assuming that our thinking should begin with the idea—it may well end there—that things are fairly well in order and only slight adjustments are needed. Some, over the years, have thought that more radical solutions were necessary.

This discussion focuses on the relation between the ideas of exit and security. To the extent that a focus is on the policies of the liberal state, the book suggests that it is useful to connect ideas of security and the issues considered in the pluralist/federalist discussions. Modern liberal states assume that exit from associations classified as "voluntary" is possible. But while "exit" is understood as possible, this exit—particularly from intense and longstanding associations—is commonly understood as the unusual and even tragic case. (An example is divorce and family breakdown).. The norm is understood as stability, and exit is the exception.

Federalist frameworks should be conceived not merely in terms of the possibility of experiment and exploration, but also should provide safety net provisions of political and welfare rights for individuals who were undertaking changes and for those who might be injured by more changes. Programs like universal basic income support the goals of individualism and security, without assuming fixed group affiliations.

If H.G. Wells said that he would not follow William Morris into utopian remaking of mankind, others were prepared to at least hope that the Soviet experiments of the 1920s and 1930s would lead to something in the way of making the "new man". John Maynard Keynes reflected the position of Webb for example, when he wrote of the Soviet world that he thought that the Soviets intended to destroy the idea that

in Family Law", *Rutgers Law Review* 40, 1093–1132, 1110.

4 Jellinek, quoted by Charles Black (1959), "The Death Penalty", *Tulane Law Rev* 51, 429–445, 434.

being someone who made money was a respectable life choice.[5] What is clear to the observer from the present day, is that this did not happen. Decades of Soviet rule and imposition of the socialist ideology did not destroy the desire for money any more than it destroyed traditional religion. Another set of modern utopians, the founders of the kibbutz movement, were also proven an unreliable model. The kibbutz has gone the way of private enterprise, and again we see that the "new man" has not been created.

But the American reformers at the time of the New Deal were not, in fact, trying to create "new men." They were only trying selectively to support some wage earners who were already there, and already maintaining a value system understood to be American. Similarly, many American reformers now are not trying to create "new men." They are trying to give free play to the impulses and choices of the men and women who exist, as they exist. The debate now, as previously, is about what to do about those whose exercise of their choices does not produce market success.

As noted, for some, like Gertrude Himmelfarb,[6] the answer to failure and poverty is devolution from the national state through various organizations down to the family. But the answer to the question she asks (Why not do it this way?) is that the mechanisms described are, from the point of view of the individual, unreliable. The family, as demonstrated in Chapter 2, has changed to such a degree that we are not even sure how to discuss it. The traditional family, which may once have had the capacity to sustain its members, was perhaps known for its beneficence and support but was surely also immortalized in the accounts of the arbitrary power exercised by one generation over another. The middle-level social groups, churches, employers, mutual aid societies, are also unreliable (from the point of view of the individual) because of the power of expulsion, a power that is intrinsic to their self-definition. It may be that there must always be a residual mechanism—the state—to support the expelled individual in the same way that there is, in the idea of citizenship, a residual definition of membership. But then it turns out that the state, the most obvious mechanism for such support, is itself unreliable. States may redefine their policies. The Soviet Union collapses. The welfare states of Europe decide that their traditional approaches are too expensive to be sustained. Moreover, individuals may have identities that are fluid, so that membership becomes a complex question.

Reinvention and Membership

There are aspects of security that may be peculiarly American. The United States is a country founded by people who left their homes and families, possibly even their wives, to establish new lives and sometimes new identities.

Reinvention of self is an American way of life. "Today is the first day of the rest of your life" is a particularly dramatic and urgent form of *carpe diem*. It signals not

5 Keynes, *Essays in Persuasion*, 302, 303.

6 Himmelfarb, Introduction to De Tocqueville, *Memoirs of Papuerism*, ibid.

only the seizing of opportunities but also the possibility of making serious change. The person who makes a new life in a new state is not an unusual figure in the United States, and they do not have to be a figure modeled on Paul Gaugin to decide that they have had enough of one life and want to try another.[7] The idea that religion is a chosen status, and that one can shift easily from one religion to another, is common place. The shifting of domestic partners and domestic arrangements is another signal of this attitude toward reinvention. Some of this has to do with the increased availability of legal divorce, but some of it is simply an aspect of the American approach to the possibility of change. If the family is one illustration of this reinvention, another is the current approach to employment, in which lifetime commitment to one company, for example, is no longer to be assumed. Adult education in the United States has meant that it is not necessary to view educational experiences of one's early 20s as setting the limits of one's adult activities. People go to school late, retrain, and re-emerge as something else. They may become professionals. They may give up professional identities to become craftsmen or entrepreneurs.

But while there is some evidence for the truth of these descriptions, our approach to security does not on the whole recognize the significance of the fluidity of identities. Our tendency is, at the moment, to conceive protection through groups. The wage earner and his family; the worker and his group plan.[8] Rather, our constructs are based on the assumption of stable embedded-ness. This will be explored first through a discussion of Daniel Defoe, and then, opening the issues of the complexity of membership, through a treatment of Harold Frederic's novel, *The Damnation of Theron Ware.*[9]

Insurance has a literature of its own and Daniel Defoe is part of it.[10] But there are other parts which are less proposals than explorations. As noted, Robert Heinlein explored the consequences of knowing precisely the date of one's death,[11] and dealt with the manipulation of the appearance of risk.[12] There are many stories in

7 See W. Somerset Maugham (1944), *The Razor's Edge* (New York: Vintage), p. 381.

8 We see "pensions" as a solution to risk. But pensions also have risks. For an indication of the different risks associated with defined benefit and defined contribution pensions, see Michael Graetz and Jerry Mashaw (1999), *True Security: Rethinking American Social Insurance* (New Haven, CT: Yale University Press). pp. 352–53, n. 19.

9 Harold Frederic (1896, 1960) *Damnation of Theron Ware* (New York: Holt Rhinehart and Winston Inc).

10 Of course, there is also a professional literature. See Spencer Kimball (1961), "The Purpose of Insurance Regulation: A Preliminary Inquiry in the Theory of Insurance Law", Minnesota Law Review 45, 471–524. Tom Baker (1996), "The Genealogy of Moral Hazard", *Texas Law Review* 75 237–292. See generally Viviana Zelizer (1979), *Morals and Markets: The Develoment of Life Insurance in the United States* (New York: Columbia University Press). Kenneth Abraham and Lance Liebman, "Private Insurance, Social Insurance and Tort Reform: Toward a new vision of compensation for illness and injury" 93 *Columbia Law Review*, 75–451, 75.

11 Heinlein, cited above.

12 Brecht, cited above.

which an insurance recovery provides the motive for a crime. All of this is about the reflections of insurance. As suggested above, a particularly important example is Lorraine Hansberry's, *Raisin in the Sun*,[13] because this play provides a perspective on life insurance that is largely omitted from the conventional treatments.

The writing of Daniel Defoe reveals, at least at times, a conventional understanding of groups, and particularly occupational groups. The life of Defoe on the other hand illustrates the fluidity of group affiliations in a way which also, from time to time, shows up in his writing. In *Robinson Crusoe*, we see a man who discusses with his father which of three classes to belong to, life having assigned him to one, but in effect only provisionally. But the character himself is a free man who becomes a slave and then a man alone on an island, who then rejoins society.

Defoe's life reveals the chameleon. The name, to begin with, is a construction. A man called Daniel Foe at the age of 35 decided to add a more aristocratic sound (De). Or perhaps, as has been suggested, a journalist involved in many arguments did not want to carry a name like "Foe." But we see in his life the sort of change in name (which was used in *Emblems of Pluralism* to signal the complex self). Further, throughout his life, we see changes in status: a man who says that he was rich and poor 13 times, a bankrupt sometimes, a merchant sometimes. Finally, a man of definitionally mixed affiliations, an intelligence agent, even a spy.[14]

Yet it is this man who, in the "Essay on Projects", concerned with problems of pensions and insurance (as in *A Journal of the Plague Year* he was concerned with issues of public health) who seems consistently to see fixed groups:

> If Mankind cou'd agree, as these might be Regulated, all things which have Casualty in them, might be Secur'd. But the one thing is Particularly requir'd in this way of Assurances; None can be admitted, but such whose Circumstances are, at least in some degree, alike, and so Mankind mut be sorted into Classes; and as their Contingences differ, every different Sort may be a Society upon even Terms; for the Circumstances of People, as to Life, differ extremely by the Age and Constitution of their Bodies, and difference of Employment; as he that lives on shore, against him that goes to Sea, or a Young Man against an Old Man; or a Shopkeeper against a Soldier, are unequal; I don't pretend to determine the Controverted Point of Predestination, the Foreknowledge and Decrees of Providence; perhaps, if a Man be Decreed to be Kill'd in the Trenches, the same Foreknowledge Order'd him to List himself a Soldier that it might come to pass; and the like of a Seaman; but this I am sure, speaking of Second Causes, a Seaman or a Soldier is subject to more contingent hazards than other Men, and therefore are not upon equal Terms to form such a Society; nor is an Annuity on the Life of such a Man worth so much as it is upon other Men; therefore if a Society shou'd agree together to Pay the Executor of every Member so much after the Decease of the said Member, the Seamens Executors wou'd most certainly have an Advantage, and receive more than they Pay. So

13 Lorraine Hansberry (1958, 1994) *A Raisin in the Sun* (New York: Vintage).

14 For discussion of a modern example, see George Steiner (1984), "The Cleric of Treason," in *George Steiner: A Reader* (Oxford: Oxford University Press), pp. 178-204, on the art historian and spy, Anthony Blunt.

that 'tis necessary to sort the World into Parcels, Seamen with Seamen, Soldiers with Soldiers, and the like. [15]

When we consider the subject of groups and security, we focus on fixed affiliations; when we think about groups and individual liberty in a liberal state, we think about changing affiliations and the necessity of mechanisms for exit.[16] This double think seems to mark much of our work.

As the Defoe example shows, such an account of fixed groups may be to be written by someone who is quite different, even like Defoe, a chameleon.

The Damnation of Theron Ware, one of the great religious novels of nineteenth-century America, shows the interaction between religious groups in a way in which the formal affiliations are as it happens fixed; but here the interior lives move and what the movement sometimes shows is that individuals do not correctly understand the issues of groups and affiliations.

To begin with, we find that the author of the *Damnation of Theron Ware*, Harold Frederic, was a traveler, an émigré, (he lived for many years in London) whose private life included two households and two families, one with his legal wife (who refused him a divorce) the other with a woman he met in England. (This woman was a Christian Scientist. When Frederic died, relatively young, her refusal to call a doctor resulted in a trial.)

His character, the Methodist minister Theron Ware is someone quite different. His affiliation is with conservative Methodism in Upper New York State. His is provincial, even bigoted. The book concerns his encounter with an Irish priest and a young woman in the priest's circle. The priest is a man of unusual sophistication and learning, quite different from Ware's image of what the Irish are like or what Catholics are like. The book is not about a conversion to Catholicism. This would make the change in group status clear. Rather it is about Ware's "illumination," his adoption, in his mind at least, of the codes of a group he does not fully understand. Theron Ware is a man who says "we" too quickly. He has, perhaps, a version of the heart too soon made glad. He claims membership in a group, which does not accept him, and in even provisionally accepting the group, he will reject another.

Is this group, to which Theron Ware aspires, to be defined in terms of religion? Ethnicity? Intelligence? Talent? How can we tell the basis of the group membership? There are four people: three men, one woman. Two men of the cloth, one pianist, one scientist. Catholics and one Methodist. Three Irish. There are also commonalities: all are Caucasian. All are American. All live in a small city in Upper New York State. All speak English. Three speak other languages and are widely read. Ware says: "I would not say this outside of our small group." But however we define the group,

---

15 *An Essay Upon Projects*. Daniel Defoe (1697) reprint. Eds Joyce Kennedy, Michael Seidel, Maximillian Novak (1999) (New York: AMS), 48–49.

16 Albert Hirschman (1970), *Exit Voice and Loyalty* (Cambridge: Harvard University Press.)

he is not in it. The others respond to him, finally by directly communicating their rejection.[17]

But there is a level at which he has a tremendous confidence. He comes from a group—conservative Methodists—described in terms of complacency. The suggestion is that the sense of salvation creates great certainty. Even at the end, when he is at his lowest point, Ware can quickly imagine a new life in the West, in which he stands in front of an admiring audience. His own limits are explained with reference to his profession. Being a minister, a person of such authority and presence, does not encourage thinking about paying bills and dealing with creditors. He himself understands his "illumination" in terms of the rejection of those who do not meet his new standard. And he moves on. It is self-reliance and self-confidence of a kind that resonates with a strand in American culture. Emerson's self-reliance insists that it is the appropriate mental stance for everyone. But self-reliance can be learned in different ways. A twentieth-century libertarian like Robert Heinlein will talk in terms of fortifying his own property and building his own bomb shelters.[18] Others will see the need for more collective solutions.

The Pillars and Utopia

Each of the three pillars of security can be discussed in terms of utopia. That the state can be built on a utopian idea is obvious, and the idealization of home and family hardly requires elaboration. "Heaven lies around us in our infancy …" Home is the haven from the heartless world," as the title of Christopher Lasch's book has it. And the religious and secular treatments of insurance can also be linked through the idea of utopia.[19] The rhetoric of utopia is invoked by writers on risk, or insurance, operating from different political orientations. Thus, Francois Ewald writes: "The 19th century's dream of security becomes a utopia of a science always ever more

17 The priest will not invariably be at home to him. Celia's farewell kiss—misunderstood—is elaborated in a speech making plain that he is not acceptable. The scientist has always been cool. Ware, who understands so little of his own world (he does not know why he was rejected for a position, or that another person is paying for his piano) understands even less of this other world. He has always lived in small places, he says, and did not know that there were different kinds of kisses.

18 Robert Heinlein, "How to be a Survivor: The art of staying alive in the atomic age", in Expanded Universe (New York: Ace Books) p. 163. For another science fiction writer's brief rebuttal to Heinlein's libertarianism, see Isaac Asimov, Great Science Fiction Stories of 1940 (eds Asimov and Martin Greenberg) (New York: Dorset Press) p. 79: if not Washington, then "it is the 'local bully on the block who will take over, and I'd rather have Washington.'"

19 "Utopia" is used here evocatively and not with definitional precision. See Lyman Tower Sargent, "Utopia: The Problem of Definition", Extrapolation, 16, 137–48.

capable of controlling risks."[20] Anthony Giddens speaks of utopian realism.[21] The idea of Utopia as substantive may also overlap with the description of Germany as Eldorado, a place of wealth and caution, as offered by Ulrich Beck.[22] Some of these descriptions see a society as a utopia in practice precisely because of insurance, and particularly state insurance.[23] Edward Bellamy conceived his future utopian state in terms of insurance. Today, from the libertarian side, Murray Rothbard, in a scheme for a future libertarian society, sees a policing role for insurance companies.[24]

We can connect insurance, family and utopia in their discrete historical incarnations. One way of suggesting the connections is to follow the lead of Morton Keller and see insurance companies as voluntary associations, alternative to the state, which provide social benefits in the same way as the family.[25] We may also invoke that smallest state, the family. The Oneida community was, as an observer said, a family of two hundred.[26] And the Metropolitan Life Insurance Company was a "family of thirty million."[27]

That is half way to solidaristic solutions that say that whether or not everyone is poor, everyone is subject to risk, and that social insurance should cover everyone. That everyone is touched by the risks of life is clear in Bellamy's famous image of the coach. It is caught in the utopian novel *Looking Backward*, in Bellamy's description

---

20 Francois Ewald (1999), "The Return of the Crafty Genius: An Outline of a Philosophy of Precaution", *Connecticut Insurance Law Journal.* 6, 47–79, 58. "While one cannot eliminate them (there is never zero risk), they will have been sufficiently reduced to be able to be dealt with collectively: accidents are the waste aspect, necessary although more marginalized, of scientific and technical progress."

21 See Anthony Giddens (1990), *The Consequences of Modernity* (Cambridge: Polity Press) 154–58.

22 See Ulrich Beck (1992), "From Industrial Society to the Risk Society; Questions on Survival, Social Structure and Ecological Enlightenment", *Theory, Culture and Society* 9, 97–123.

23 Another view might be that in utopia no insurance would ever be needed.

24 See Murray N. Rothbard (1989), *For a New Liberty: The Libertarian Manifesto* (New York: Libertarian Review Foundation) pp. 217–19. Some libertarian arguments reject insurance. See, for example, Ludwig Von Mises (1951), *Socialism: An Economic and Sociological Analysis*, pp. 475–8. Von Mises writes: "Social insurance has thus made the neurosis of the insured a dangerous public disease. Should the institution be extended and developed, the disease will spread. No reform can be of any assistance. We cannot weaken or destroy the will to health without producing illness" (p. 478).

25 See generally Morton Keller (1963), *The Life Insurance Enterprise, 1885–1910: A Study in the Limits of Corporate Power* (Cambridge: Belknap Press of Harvard Unversity Press).

26 See Carol Weisbrod (1980), *The Boundaries of Utopia* (New York: Pantheon Books) p. 177. (T.W. Higginson referred to the Oneida community as "a family of two hundred living in apparent harmony and among the comforts which associated life secures." Ibid.)

27 Louis I. Dublin (1943), *A Family of Thirty Million* (New York: Metropolitan Life Insurance).

of the human condition as a coach on which some sat while others pulled the coach. The role of risk and accident is explicitly put on the description of the coach.

"By the rule of the coach a man could leave his seat to whom he wished, but on the other hand there were many accidents by which it might at any time be wholly lost." Then they would "help to drag the coach on which they had before ridden so pleasantly." The result was that "the apprehension that this might happen to them or their friends was a constant cloud upon the happiness of those who rode."[28] But who are they? One answer is "it might be any of us." Thus, the ACLU book *Rights of the Poor* (1974) said that most Americans are at some point or another, poor.[29] The change in marital status, which results in impoverishment of women and children, was, in part, a matter of class drop.[30] This impoverishment did not meet the tests of absolute poverty, but it is a change in status and condition that has serious consequences.

Utopian thinking on poverty and state continues, of course, and some of it concerns the pillars of security. The Australian political theorist Robert Goodin makes some of the central points. He begins by noting:

> Social security famously rests on four pillars: the state, the market, the family and the community. Econocrats at the World Bank and Organization for Economic Cooperation and Development remind us of that fact, hoping to persuade the state to step back and leave more space for those sectors to shoulder a larger share of the burden.

He continues by reviewing the connections that are the foundation of this book:

> Whatever else we say for or against such welfare reforms, all the cutbacks in state provision mentioned above rest crucially on the assumption that the other three pillars—the family, the market, the community—are actually capable of bearing more of the weight. That, I suggest is radically untrue. All of those other pillars are themselves crumbling at the same time as the state pillar is being chipped away.[31]

(Goodin thinks that the family is "crumbling." The argument here is that it is changing its function, doing some things better than previously, some things worse.) In short, Goodin concludes:

> The state, then, is backing out of the business of social welfare provision at the same time as the other classic pillars of social security are being eroded. All the pillars are collapsing at once, for all too many people. Not everyone, to be sure: many people are still blest with

---

28 Edward Bellamy (1966[1888]), *Looking Backward* (ed. Robert C. Elliot) (Boston, MA: Houghton Mifflin), p. 7.

29 Sylvia Law (1974), *Rights of the Poor* (New York: Avon).

30 Barbara Ehrenreich (1989) *Fear of Falling* (New York: Harper Collins).

31 Robert Goodin (1994), *World Bank, Averting the Old Age Crisis* (New York, Oxford: University Press for the World Bank); Organisation for Economic Cooperation and Development (1997), *Family, Market and Community* (Paris: OECD). Robert E. Goodin. (2000) "Crumbling Pillars: Social Security Futures" 71 *The Political Quarterly* 144–150.

> stable marriages, caring kin and communities, secure employment and comfortable benefit entitlements. But increasing numbers of people are suffering increasing insecurities on all those fronts. For them, market, family and community pillars prove to be woefully inadequate substitutes for reduced state provision for social security.

Goodin describes a number of proposed solutions and then makes a basic point:

> My larger point, however, is that any of those unconditional benefit schemes would be better suited to the increasingly non-standardized world towards which we are moving. Let us simply give up, not only on means-testing, but on conditionality of any other form. Let us simply give everyone a fair share of social resources, and allow them to arrange their own affairs as they will. A utopian vision it may be, but some utopias have a way of coming true; and if my diagnosis of our present plight is even remotely correct, the increasing non-standardization of our social world will eventually drive us towards one or the other of the futures which I have been sketching here. It is up to us to decide whether it is to be utopia or dystopia.[32]

Richard Epstein,[33] in his book, *Mortal Peril*, an argument against universal health care, lays out the assumptions of his system. Stressing scarcity first, he distinguishes between those approaches that are built on wealth maximization and those that focus more on welfare entitlements. In the course of the presentation, he notes that, of course, no one would argue for poverty. But in fact some people have argued for poverty, meaning voluntary poverty. Individuals have from time to time rejected the proposition that acquisition was the way to the good life. Thus, Dorothy Day of the Catholic Workers movement, called ordinary poverty "destitution" and thought that the world would be better if more people adopted voluntary poverty as a principle. So too Gandhi. And certainly many have made the claim that materialism, consumerism, and accumulations were not the highest values. There are some calls for the simple life now associated with the life of those who live on social security alone, and, as noted below, there is an odd echo of the rejection of the acquisitive life in some of the models offered to today's senior citizens. We sometimes see a picture today of the elderly living on social security as people living frugally, carefully, happily, though their only income is the present social security system. Thus, under the title "Simply Living", the AARP (Association for the Advancement of Retired Persons) has an article subtitled "meet four Americans who manage to live on social Security alone, and you know what? They're doing just fine, thank you."[34] Their lives are presented as full and good. They do not, it is suggested, suffer even though they are not committed to the consumption values of the mainstream culture.

---

32 Goodin; See also Goodin's essay in Philippe Van Parijs (ed) *What's Wrong with a Free Lunch?* (Boston: Beacon Press) (Robert E. Goodin, "Something for Nothing", 90-97)

See also Goodin's discussion in Van Parijs (ed) (1992), *Arguing for Basic Income* (London: Verso) "Towards a Presumptuous Social Welfare Policy" 195–214.

33 Richard Epstein (1999) *Moral Peril* (Cambridge: Perseus Books).

34 William Newcott (2005), "Simply Living", AARP, May.

So at least for the elderly, we can imagine another sort of life and call it decent. It is the simple life and it is not, of course, a life that everyone would want, but it is a life that some Americans at least find acceptable and even desirable. As to social security, that level of provision for the elderly—do we think them "poor"?—has seemed acceptable for Americans and it may be possible that it will prove acceptable for others. It is the life imagined by those who support a minimum income allowance as a guarantee for everyone.

"The poor ye have always with you,"[35] is, we are told by Jim Wallis, the best-known biblical verse on poverty, read as though there was no reason to do anything to remedy the condition.[36] Wallis asks: How do modern Americans interpret this text? "We simply use it as an excuse. 'The poor you will always have with you' gets translated into 'There is nothing we can do *about* poverty,' and the poor will always be there, so why bother?" Yet that's not what the text is saying at all. The critical difference between Jesus' disciples and a middle-class church is precisely this: our lack of proximity to the poor. The continuing relationship to the poor that Jesus assumes will be natural for his disciples is unnatural to an affluent church. The "social location" of the affluent Christians has changed; we are no longer "with" the poor, and they are no longer with us. The middle-class church doesn't know the poor and they don't know us. Wealthy Christians talk about the poor but have no friends who are poor. So they merely speculate on the reasons for their condition, often placing the blame on the poor themselves." Self-reliance would suggest that the poor should help themselves.[37]

The American reformers of the early part of the twentieth century were concerned about the working man, as Rubinow would have put it. The New Deal was a program for some of the lower classes. The upper classes were assumed to be largely taken care of, by their own assets, or by private insurance.

The picture looks somewhat different in the early data of the twenty-first century in the United States. While the emphasis on the lower classes (now heavily minorities) is unchanged for the reformers—and if anything becomes more intense under the pressure of the idea that the gap between rich and poor gets larger—the pressure on the rich to stay rich has become more intense. They perceive their security as threatened in a new way.

Employment for life, tenure at one company for decades, a comfortable retirement funded by the company to which one has been loyal, a passing on of money and status to one's children, none of this is taken for granted. Descriptions of the anxieties of the middle and even upper-middle class make plain that if we are thinking of psychological insecurity, those who "have" may be as insecure as those who "have not." Theirs is the anxiety of the passengers on Bellamy's coach. Moreover, they are,

35 Matthew 26:11.

36 Jim Wallis (2005), *God's Politics: How the Right Gets it Wrong and the Left Doesn't Get It* (New York/San Francisco: Harper) , p. 211.

37 Jim Wallis.

it seems, unlikely to produce a more complete security for themselves by rethinking or restructuring their lives or their possessions.

"They're having unauthorized fantasies about a simpler life, but we're going to remind them what's at stake. We're going to rattle their golden handcuffs until we've dispelled all doubt. There is no exit strategy." The writer describes the investment of the middle and upper middle class high-salaried worker. "They've invested too many sleepless nights and frayed nerves and lost opportunities. They've sold their friends and family on Deferred-Life. And they're fully vested in *our* definition of success. To change that definition is to lose everything—money, respect, and your Elite Status in our Preferred-Customer program." This does not turn someone into a non-person. "Of course, the successful people may still be polite to you, but they won't pay quite so much attention – they'll always be looking over your shoulder."[38]

Successful Americans do not usually lay their accomplishments as resulting from anything other than their own individual characteristics. They see American society as meritocratic. Since they achieved their own success; other people must be getting their just desserts.[39] Judith Warner focused on the impact of this culture on the family, and notes particularly high stress mothering. She quotes Kevin Phillips, author of *Wealth and Democracy: A Political History of the American Rich.* Phillips labeled this change the "financialization" of American corporate culture. It was a new moral order:

> A new value system, characterized by a kind of survival-of-the-fittest mentality, which permeated every aspect of our society. If you weren't at the top, earning the most and buying the best (even of such basic human services as health care and education), then it had to be because you weren't good enough to be there. And so, if you were saddled with crumbling public schools and could afford no better doctors than the second-rate ones provided through your HMO [Health Maintenance Organization], you were simply getting what you deserved.[40]

Others have spoken of the same thing with an emphasis on the family.

> The downsizing of the 1990s were a wake-up call. The social compact—You do your job well and you stay employed—is dead, at least for the time being. Jobs were destroyed and lives were ruined, but one message came through loud and clear: Employment insecurity is the new way of life, even during time of low unemployment. Many workers have begun to rethink their commitment to employers, because their employers have changed their commitment to them. The extra sacrifice of missed family birthdays because of long hours

---

38 Richard Florida (2002) *The Rise of the Creative Class* (New York: Perseus) p. 158, quoting someone in Austin, Texas.

39 James Loewen (1996) *Lies My Teacher Told Me* (New York: Simon and Schuster) p. 306.

40 Kevin Phillips quoted in Judith Warner's (2005), *Perfect Madness* (New York: Riverhead Books) p. 199.

> at the office no longer makes sense, and maybe never did. As the old saying goes, people on their deathbeds never wish they had spent more time at the office.[41]

The proposals for flex time and split jobs may come back to the domestic table, but they are not in the corporate table.

While golden parachutes for CEOs may help here (for very few), private insurance probably will not, altogether; certainly not about unhappiness at work, and not in relation to the problem of skills no longer needed or changes in the market value of a house. When we speak of the limits of insurance, we are sometimes talking about the fact that the middle-class and the upper-middle class cannot by insurance protect their assets against inflation or market drop. Robert Shiller's proposals to the effect that one should be able to insure all risks tends to address specifically the risks faced by those who have wealth at risk.[42]

Upward mobility in America has meant that some who are upper-middle class did not begin that way. Their sense of possibility, up and down, is necessarily different from those who see a naturalness in how they were born and raised and who have never experienced dislocation. It is that second group that may have a failure of imagination. The first group has its own memories.

> And the poor feel insecure. Here is a comparison that is international in focus: Not only is their income uncertain—changes in economic circumstances beyond their control can lead to lower real wages and a loss of jobs, dramatically illustrated by the East Asia crisis—but they face health risks and continual threats of violence, sometimes from other poor people trying against all odds to meet the needs of their family, sometimes from police and other in positions of authority. While those in developed countries fret about the inadequacies of health insurance, those in developing countries must get by without any form of insurance …"[43]

But the description of New Orleans in 2005 as "Third World" remind us that the description may be apt for certain parts of the United States.

As to artists, we are familiar with the idea that some would sacrifice certain aspects of life in favor of the opportunity to produce unprofitable work. Beethoven had complained about the necessity of earning a living and wanted a kind of bank for composers.[44] Others have taken "day" jobs, Wallace Stevens, Charles Ives, Franz

---

41 Joanne Ciulla quoted in Richard Florida, *The Rise of the Creative Class*, pp. 109–10.

42 Robert Shiller, *New Economic Order* (Princeton: Princeton University Press). The classes of the classless society have been described from time to time with striking acuteness. Paul Fussell's *Class* remains a useful guide to the American class structure. Fiction provides a guide to the values of different classes, despite the insistence of those (like Hoover) who see America as classless. Jonathan Franzen's, *The Corrections*, for example, describes the "poor think" of parts of the Mid-West.

43 Joseph E. Stiglitz (2002) *Globalization and Its Discontents* (New York: W.W. Norton & Company), p. 83.

44 Beethoven's letters, cited above.

Kafka in insurance companies. But what if one had the option to live modestly in "decent poverty"[45] without a day job?

A certain qualification, therefore, must be introduced into the discussion when we say that individuals may not agree. More significantly, perhaps, at least as a political matter, is the idea that entire cohorts or generations might not see accumulation and acquisition as a prime good. It is a possibility opened by the discussions of generations that assume that large groups of people, shaped in significant ways by their shared life experiences, deviate from the value systems held by the groups immediately preceding and following them.[46]

But we are, in the United States, accustomed to a discussion in which the American Way of Life (something that once had to do with ideas of the rule of law, democracy, openness, tolerance) have come to mean something about a standard of living. The Way of Life becomes the Life Style. A discussion of a minimum income seems, initially, to make little sense in this context because so little money could not assure the aspiration of the millions for the American Life Style. (Rubinow's response to this, given in 1930, was that the principle of a comfortable old age should take precedence over the principle of the second car for every family or a victrola in every home.)[47] Here, a fictional treatment of the importance of a small stipend may be useful. To begin with, as in the life and development of Larry, in Somerset Maugham's *The Razor's Edge*, is premised on the point that inheritances can be important even when they are small. The income that Larry will receive from his inheritance is so small that his fiancée will not go forward with him until he abandons his plan to read and study and instead goes for a job like everyone else. But the small inheritance is sufficient for the likes of the scholar. And later, the stipend will be defended as a source of Larry's freedom. But finally, much later in his spiritual development, Larry comes to see the money as a burden, and he gives it away. He would choose the life of the mendicant priest if he could, but sees that there is no place for the begging bowl in the United States. Americans assume that everyone will work, and so he will, also, despite his individual aspirations. Larry's development seems to show that.

A final assumption to be explored is the nature of the individual. And the discussions tend to assume static wills. Individuals have fluid wills and fluid identities.[48]

The proposal for a social dividend is one of those that is consistent with libertarian thinking, and tries to open a level of choice presently unavailable.[49] It

---

45 See Dorothy Day, *Loaves and Fishes* (San Francisco: Harper and Row).

46 See William Strauss and Neil Howe (1991), *Generations: History of America's Future, 1584–2069*. (New York: Quill, William Morrow).

47 I.M. Rubinow (1930) "The Modern Problem", in I.M. Rubinow (ed.) *The Modern Problem of the Care of the Aged* (proceedings of the Deutsch foundation conference, Chicago), pp. 1–14.

48 This expands a discussion in the final chapter of Weisbrod, *Emblems of Pluralism*.

49 For detailed arguments see, inter alia, Phillipe Van Parijs (1992), *Arguing for Basic Income* (London: Verso); Phillipe Van Parijs (1995), *Real Freedom for All* (Oxford:

is often defended as a plan that does much more than providing a way to deal with poverty. An unconditional universal income is defended as resulting in the good society for all members.[50]

Thus, Erich Fromm: "A guaranteed income, which becomes possible in the era of economic abundance, could for the first time free man from the threat of starvation, and thus make him truly free and independent from any economic threat. Nobody would have to accept conditions of work merely because he otherwise would be afraid of starving; a talented or ambitious man or woman could learn new skills to prepare himself or herself for a different kind of occupation." Fromm is aware of gender issues: "A woman could leave her husband," and also issues of adolescence, since with an income, an adolescent could leave his family. People would learn to be no longer afraid, if they did not have to fear hunger. (This holds true, of course, only if there is also no political threat that inhibits man's free thought, speech, and action.)"[51]

"Utopia" or "dystopia," the usual opposition, is not the only contrast we want. While one convention distinguishes utopia from the real world, so that an acre in Middlesex is better than a principality in Utopia,[52] another sees that utopia is something to be achieved in the world. In the American setting, this approached a vision of progress that linked those Christian post millenialists—and, those who call themselves progressives or secular reformers. While certain real life proposals are called utopian—meaning that they are visionary, or unrealistic—that is a comment about the likelihood of success, not about the real context of the objectives. Utopian proposals are often directed at the world. The nineteenth-century American utopias were of this type, communities in the world that provided models of the good, all but perfect life. But, the very idea of community has also in it a different kind of link to risk, hazard, insecurity, and, in fact, everything we summarize in the words "After the Fall."

Another contrast therefore is to Eden. In the Eden of affluence[53] "there would be no economic goods. … all goods would be free, like sand in the desert or water at the beach. But no society has reached a utopia of limitless possibility. Goods are limited while wants seem infinite." As to the United States, the classic text book notes: "Even in the United States, production is simply not high enough to meet everyone's desires. Our national output would have to be many times larger before the average American could live at the level of the average doctor of lawyer." (And of course, the

Clarendon).

50 See Van Parijs, *Arguing for a Basic Income*. Ackerman and Alstott define it as "far below subsistence—level income" (p. 210) But this is not necessary (Van Parijs).

51 Erich Fromm (1966), "The Psychological Aspect of a Guaranteed Income", in Robert Theobald (ed.) *The Guaranteed Income: Next Step in Economic Evolution* (New York: Theobald, Doubleday & Co) pp. 175–84.

52 See Lord Macaulay (1860), *Critical, Historical, and Miscellaneous Essays*. (Cambridge: Sheldon), 460. Lord Bacon, Essay: 289–410.

53 Paul A. Samuelson and William D. Nordhaus (1995), *Economics*, 15th edition. (New York: McGraw Hill), p. 4.

book notes, outside the United States one finds material deprivation. But, they seem to assume, not inside the United States.)[54]

But this was not Eden. First, of course, if the "want" was to eat of the tree of knowledge, this was forbidden. And second, in a world in which there was a harmony between human wants and nature, the issue would not be fulfilling all wants but rather a perfect correspondence between what was wanted and what was provided.

Some current wants, in short, are either manufactured or are a response to a fallen world. Pufendorf made the point in his discussion of natural law. Pufendorf noted:

> in this our present state there are a large number of affirmative precepts which seem to have had no place in the primeval state. This is partly because they presuppose institutions which (for all that we know) did not exist in mankind's condition of felicity; and partly because they are unintelligible without poverty and death, which were foreign to that state. For example, we now have among the precepts of natural law: do not deceive anyone in buying and selling; do not use false length, weight or measure; return borrowed money at the agreed time. But we have not yet clearly resolved the question whether, if the human race had continued without sin, we would practise the kind of commerce that we now practise, and whether there would have been any use for money. Similarly, if states as they now exist had no place in the condition of innocence, there would also have been no room there for precepts which assume the existence of states of that kind and the power of government contained in them. We are also now bidden by natural law to help the poor, to come to the aid of those stricken by undeserved disaster and to care for widows and orphans. Yet it is irrelevant to address these precepts to those who are not liable to poverty, destitution and death.[55]

Further, one might consider the idea of John Winthrop[56] in *A Model of Christian Charity* that in the City on a Hill of the New England Puritans, some people's necessities should be met by other people forgoing luxuries. It is an idea we see still. And of course it was part of the thinking of I.M. Rubinow.

And there we see a very special kind of security. There seems to be no risk in Eden, except the risk of expulsion. Eden, the home of man before the Fall, is a place without struggle, with necessity, without death. After the Fall, men must work by the sweat of their brows.[57] It is an idea we have trouble getting away from. Though Herbert Spencer is sometimes identified as secular, for example, one who left the evangelical dissenting Christianity of his youth behind him, in his first article he

---

54 Ibid.

55 Samual Pufendorf, (ed, Tully, 1991) *On the Duty of Man and Citizen According to Natural Law* (Cambridge: Cambridge University Press) p. 12.

56 John Winthrop's 1630 speech, composed on the Arabella while sailing to the Massachusetts Bay Colony is one of the classics of American religious and political literature. The reference to the colony as a "city on a hill" has been quoted frequently by American politicians.

57 See Spencer's use of this in his essay on the Poor Law in Herbert Spencer (2001[1994]), *Political Writings* (ed. John Offer) (Cambridge: Cambridge University Press), Appendix to Spencer's article of 1836 on the Poor Law, pp. 177–181.

was still able to speak of the "truth of scriptures."[58] He argued from the language of the bible relating to work. The article to which he responded advocated "the right of people to live ultimately without toil and exertion, whilst at the same time they should receive from the national stock, comparatively sufficient means to render them comfortable." Spencer said:

> Do you, then, deny or, have you forgotten, those declarations: 'in the sweat of thy face shalt thou eat bread' "six days shalt thou labour" "if any will not work neither let him eat." The whole system of man's responsibility, and of his future reward or punishment, depending upon his being "diligent in business, fervent in sprit, serving the Lord" seems completely set aside by your reasoning.[59]

Eden is a place of a perfect relation between the human being and the creator, which is in the end a relation of trust. If we use the C.S. Lewis description of Eden in *Perelandra*, we see a world in which the proposition that the creator will provide for his creatures is taken to be literally true. The disobedience with which the lady is tempted in that novel is explicitly described in terms of control and human autonomy. The human creature is not to sleep on the fixed land exactly because that would mean the calculated approach to the future and a denial of the posture of dependence (compare Morelly's emphasis on dailyness.) Religious opposition to insurance can be conceived as an attempt to invoke the values of Eden, a situation that is basically that of perfect trust, as it was in the original garden. But, aside from these ideas, there is not much we know about that garden, which, like other inexplicable wonders, cannot really be described in detail. Only an atmosphere can be evoked.[60]

Utopias, by contrast, usually assumed a fallen world in which issues of security are very large. The plans for the perfect society must, in fact, resolve fundamental questions relating to need, illness and death. The human beings in that society, far from being innocent and without sin, are typically vulnerable and sometimes much worse.

For the most part, we believe that self-help—short of greed—is appropriate. That issue is replaced by ideas of welfare and the obligation of charity. (Even the most modern arguments of our state policy relating to the poor consider charity.)

---

58 Spencer, Poor Laws.

59 Poor Laws.

60 The Utopia of Cockaigne saw itself as superior to paradise (A.L. Morton (1952, 1969) *The English Utopia* [[The Land of Cokaygne]] pp. 279–285). That emphasis on dailyness also can be linked to a secure environment that is viewed negatively because it lacks freedom. Thus Hiram Bingham, the modern discoverer of Machu Picchu, had explained the absence of theft among the Incas. There were no locks on the doors, but only a little stick across the opening, signaling that the occupants were not at home. The Incas had a benevolent despotism, Bingham said, "where no one was allowed to go hungry or naked, where everyone was told what to do and when to do it, and where everything of importance belonged to the ruler. There was no object in attempting to acquire the personal possessions of others, nor was there any incentive to acquire anything which was not in daily use." Hiram Bingham (2005[1952]), *Lost City of the Incas*. Phoenix: London), p. 34.

One might say that in a situation of ordinary security, the few episodes of acute insecurity are perceived as enormous, whether these relate to hurricanes or terrorism.

The contrast is to the situation that obtained through most of human history, in which ordinary life was chronically and even desperately insecure. The history of life expectancy of infants can be used to tell the story. It is only in this most recent past that human beings routinely expect their children to live and to be raised to adulthood.

In response to this chronic insecurity, social and political institutions are developed, and two of these, the family and insurance, are the subject of the book of which this chapter is a part. One cannot, after the Fall, imagine a world without certain insecurity. H.G. Wells' *A Modern Utopia* is clear on the point. The most one can do is contain, or manage it, in schemes that will be considered more or less utopian, depending on who is doing the evaluating.

But while part of the argument about mechanisms for security is about support for those in need, those whose deprivation is pronounced, beneath the level at which others can simply walk away, another part of the argument is about change in status. And here there is a problem. A part of the free market economic argument is that a truly free market does not, as Von Mises puts it, protect vested interests.[61] One has no entitlement under the market for things to continue as they are. This is, of course, what insurance attempts to do, to the extent that it is possible. Various governmental interventions may protect the poor outside the market.[62]

The effort to engage in practical politics, to get somehow closer to "there," may involve people in difficulties and contradictions.[63] David Friedman notes that he was criticized for supporting vouchers in one chapter of his book, while opposing any government and any taxes (and any vouchers) in another. But of course the answer, he said, was that one starts within the limits of what the system now does. Vouchers would get closer to the world he wanted.[64]

Other problems may be raised by the problem that every political choice involves a conclusion on many issues. At some point, one issue may become the largest. Thus, Robert Heinlein's early work endorses social credit, and the social dividend, the minimum sustenance amount paid to every individual.[65] Later, he was a Goldwater republican. One explanation is that the issue of war with the Soviet Union had become the largest one for him.[66] Another might be that he had abandoned social credit. Another might be that he accepted it in theory but not soon and saw no point

---

61 Von Mises (1949, 1963) *Human Action* (San Francisco: Fox and Wilkes)..

62 Hayek indicated that governments, acting outside the market, could provide subsidies for the poor. See Chapter 4 above.

63 For the rich egalitarian see G.A. Cohen (2000), *If You're an Egalitarian, How Come You're so Rich?* (Cambridge, MA: Harvard University Press), p. 150.

64 David Friedman (1989, 2nd ed) *The Machinery of Freedom* (LaSalle Illinois: Open Court) XI–XII.

65 Robert Heinlein (2004) *For Us, the Living* (New York: Scribners).

66 See essays on Russia in Heinlein, *The Expanded Universe* (New York: Ace Books)

in advancing it, having moved to a point at which what interested him was the possibility of self-help within a given society.[67] Heinlein was a science fiction writer and engineer. His libertarianism reaches audiences far beyond the university. He can be linked to other libertarians who reach different audiences. (David Friedman, son of Milton Friedman, dedicated a book (*The Machinery of Freedom*) to Hayek, Milton Freidman and Robert Heinlein). He remains widely read.

Edith Wharton wrote: "One of the chief advantages of being rich was that one need not be exposed to unforeseen contingencies: by the use of ordinary firmness and common sense one could make sure of doing exactly the same thing every day at the same hour."[68] This linkage of the idea of avoidance of unforeseen contingencies, wealth, and a rigid and stultifying sense of life possibilities marks a particular critique of the utopian idea. It is not only that it is impossible. It is that it is, finally, boring. The same observation might be made of certain visions of Eden. There is a great deal of harmony but very little excitement.[69] (And indeed, there is little of specific blue prints in our description of heaven. We are more explicit about our visions of hell, which may also be more interesting and dramatic.)

While we are familiar with H.G. Wells's description of some of the anti-aesthetic characteristics of Beatrice Webb—the wife of the Bailey couple in the *New Machiavelli* who would reject live trees in favor of cut outs—we recall less frequently the indictment of Sidney Webb, a man who could "do nothing with ideas but remember and discuss them."[70] Thus legal academics in the United States are well known for proposing solutions of various kinds to real world problems and indeed scholarship lacking this normative aspect is considered weak for that reason.

Cass Sunstein argues that "*an individualistic culture, one that is firmly committed to capitalist institutions, can also accept the Second Bill of Rights, and do so in the name of individualism itself.* This in fact was one of Roosevelt's principal claims. The very idea of a second bill arose from the American experience in the early decades of the twentieth century. For this very reason, it is hard to argue that the second bill is fatally inconsistent with American culture. As we shall see, in the 1960s, the Supreme Court came close to interpreting the Constitution to recognize social and economic rights—a development that complicates the view that American culture repudiates such rights."[71] At the same time, he acknowledges the force of the law/economics arguments when he says that solution would open market solutions and be suitably attentive to issues of incentives. One cannot ignore the competing ideologies of the academic discussion.

67 The theme of much of the fiction.

68 Edith Wharton, "Souls Belated", in *Collected Stories of Edith Wharton, 1891–1950*. (ed. Maureen Howard) (New York: Library of America), pp. 95–122.

69 See George Orwell (ed. Peter Davison (1998)) *Complete Works* Vol. 16 (1943–1944) [attributed] "Can Socialists be Happy?" by John Freeman pp. 37–43, noting that heaven is "as great a flop as utopia."

70 H.G. Wells (2002[1910]), *The New Machiavelli*.(Thirsk: House of Stratus), p. 202.

71 Cass Sunstein (2004), *The Second Bill of Rights* (New York: Basic Books), p. 106.

The Ackerman/Alstott discussion in *The Stakeholder Society* engages the arguments of liberals and libertarians, but not the arguments of those who, for example, believe that the poor are being punished for sins, or that what happens, in general, in this world is not important since what counts is what happens in the next.

But "the normative" can take many forms. Some will propose a statute of a reform, and some will address government, like the advocates of the basic income discussed above. Others, like Nicholas Taleb, will address the news media, urging them to report events in a way that brings people closer to the statistical heart of things rather than the anecdotal and emotional heart, in the interest of more accurate risk assessment.[72] And some will be interested in scientific research directed not merely to security but to immortality. Eden and the Golden Age were worlds without insecurity. Hesiod (*Works and Days*) records that:

> The race of men that the immortals who dwell on Olympus made first of all was of gold. They were in the time of Kronos, when he was king in heaven; and they lived like gods, with carefree heart, remote from toil and misery. Wretched old age did not affect them either, but with hands and feet ever unchanged they enjoyed themselves in feasting, beyond all ills, and they died as if overcome by sleep. All good things were theirs, and the grain-giving soil bore its fruits of its own accord in unstinted plenty, while they at their leisure harvested their fields in contentment amid abundance. Since the earth covered up that race, they have been divine spirits by great Zeus' design, good spirits on the face of the earth, watchers over mortal men, bestowers of wealth: such is the kingly honour that they received.[73]

But if we do not resolve the issues of security, we are likely to find that immortality, and even longevity, will benefit only some.

An episode in Martha Gellhorn's early fiction called *The Trouble I've Seen* describes an interview between the wife of an unemployed worker and a "relief lady", from City Hall. The wife closes the door so that her husband won't hear the conversation. "He is taking all this very hard," she says. "Yes, I know. It is hard," the relief lady comments, and then moves on to business:

> "Now would you mind telling me Mrs. Hines, have you any life insurance, you or your husband?"
>
> "No."
>
> "Have you any relatives who could help you now?"
>
> "No."

---

72 Nicholas Taleb, "Scaring Us Senseless", July 24, 2005, *New York Times*, Sec. 4. p. 13.

73 Hesiod (1988), *Theogony and Works and Days: A New Translation* (trans. M.L. West). (1998, 1990) (Oxford/New York: Oxford University Press), p. 40.

The relief lady, representing local assistance, offers help but it is not enough to keep the couple in their house or to have them receive support with any sort of dignity.[74]

Rubinow referred often to dignity and humiliation. And it is common as a theme today. Thus Ackerman and Alstott refer several times to the issue of dignity as against social embarrassment. "Will the typical American be able to hold her head up when she retires? Will every appearance in public be an occasion for embarrassment?"[75]

With Gellhorn's depression picture of the relief lady doing an interview, we are back to the discussion of Frans Hals, standing in front of the regentesses of the Haarlem Almshouse in seventeenth-century Holland. We have moved up several hundred years, but the issues of dignity are the same.

---

74 Martha Gellhorn (1936) *The Trouble I've Seen* (New York: William Morrow), pp. 122–3.

75 Bruce Ackerman and Anne Alstott (1999), *The Stakeholder Society* (Yale University Press) p. 153.

Conclusion

This book has focused on family, private insurance and government as sources of individual security and has argued that each of these is weaker as a source of security than is often understood. The book has also argued that the linkages between these are strong, and that each source of support has built into it a view of the other sources. No one of these sources is without problems or risks. Many of these risks are familiar. We are aware, as a culture, of separate issues: the impact of divorce on the economic security of women and children, the possibility that inflation can destroy private savings, that government after some time of meeting commitments may limit its support of the elderly and the poor, that private insurance companies may look for reasons not to pay rather than reasons to pay. But the issues are often not discussed together. And it is only by bringing them together that individuals can decide questions concerning their futures. Realistic self-help requires an understanding of the limits of all these institutions. As citizens voting—if they vote—individuals may engage in single issue voting. On the question of future security—of illness, accident, old age—the individual making some decisions privately is likely to invest in more than one mechanism. To save, or not, to buy insurance or not, to rest on social security or not. The yes–no option is there, but so too are options based on fractional simultaneous investments. This book has attempted to provide some perspective on some choices.

In effect, the book has juxtaposed different forms of individual investment with a description focused on risks. Investment is a word we often limit to the financial investments of the rich, but of course this usage only describes a part of the phenomenon. We invest financially, and emotionally, in different sorts of institutions, and we rely for our security on different institutions. A recent detective novel has a representative of the Ivy League elites saying that he and other stockholders are trying to "recoup our losses." And the response from the group of former employees working with him to defeat the malfeasors is: "Us too." The first speaker is surprised. "*You* invested?" "Everything … life insurance. Health insurance. Pension plan."[1] Donald Westlake reminds us of the various forms of reliance and investments. So does Nicholas Taleb, who asks us to remember not only that there are many forms of investment besides the American stock market but also that many of them fail:

> Consider the fate of those who, in place of spending their money buying expensive toys and paying for ski trips, bought Lebanese lira denominated Treasury bills (as my grandfather did), or junk bonds from Michael Milken (as many of my colleagues in the 1980s did). Go back in history and imagine the accumulator buying Russian Imperial bonds bearing the

1 Donald Westlake (2005[2004]), *The Road to Ruin* (New York: Warner), p. 53.

> signature of Czar Nicholas II and trying to accumulate further by cashing them from the Soviet government, or Argentine real estate in the 1930s (as my great grandfather did).[2]

Presumably people who see themselves as having invested in human relationships that fail sequentially have a parallel narrative of failed investments.

The decisions each individual makes today are, at least in theory and often in fact, informed to a degree almost unknown a short time ago. Medical decisions,[3] financial decisions, personal decisions are all made in an environment of information, and often, information overload. What we don't receive through books newspapers and television we get through Google and the Internet. But our "information" is often skewed. What isn't advertising may often be advocacy. And even when a single story is more or less reliable, the connections between things are concealed or ignored. Words are used as though they had constant meanings over centuries, and the downside of programs and structures we rely on are often unknown, even to those promoting them.

Looking for solutions to social problems, some are tempted to go to writing descriptive of the state of things in Eden, or after the Messiah, for suggestions as to details. But there is not a vast amount of detailed guidance to be found there, it seems. We have certain pictures, in the Golden Age of Hesiod, the houris of the Muslims,[4] the no-marriage of St Paul, the "all things in common" of the Apostles, and, in fiction, attempts at description from the peace and harmony (before the Fall) in the floating islands of Perelandra to the domestic tensions between Adam and Eve in Mark Twain.

But the material is in general nowhere near as explicit as our blueprints for utopia or our visions of Hell. At the same time, there is something in Jewish messianic speculation that it is appropriate to invoke here.

"Let no one think that in the days of the Messiah any of the laws of nature will be set aside," Maimonides said, or that "any innovation be introduced into creation. The world will follow its normal course. They will all accept the true religion, and will neither plunder nor destroy, and together with Israel earn a comfortable living in a legitimate way." That is, we have an expulsion from Eden, and one lives by the sweat of one's brow, and also a vision of the time After the Messiah, which turns out to mean that earning a decent living is easier.[5] It is quite a modest goal, something

2 Nassim Nicholas Taleb, (2004) *Fooled by Randomness: The Hidden Role of Chance in the Markets and in Life*, 2nd edition. (New York: Thompson).

3 For an argument against the ways that through ideas of informed consent and patient decision making we put pressure on those who would prefer to place certain decisions in other hands, see Carl Schneider, *The Practice of Autonomy* (New York: Oxford).

4 In the Islamic tradition, the houris are the beautiful virgins who are associated with paradise.

5 "In that era there will be neither famine nor war, neither jealousy nor strife. Blessings will be abundant, comforts within the reach of all. The one preoccupation of the whole world will be to know the Lord. Hence Israelites will be very wise, they will know the things that are now concealed and will attain an understanding of their Creator to the utmost capacity of the

like the idea of a religious woman in Marilynne Robinson's *Housekeeping*[6] who sees Heaven as involving a reunion with her dead husband without concerns about money and in a somewhat milder climate.

But the fact that the idea of Heaven can be linked to a vision of freedom from economic anxiety based on a good job shows how far most of the world has always been from a life based on security. And in the United States particularly, we have tended to exaggerate the security provided even by the strongest of our attempts at security.

Economist George Stigler suggested that compassion for the underling would lead to a lot of injustice being done to rich people. Stigler noted that sympathy was a problem. "The compassion for the harshly treated readily overwhelms our sense of justice: the society would willingly add to the injustices heaped upon a millionaire if thereby the meager lot of an undeserving pauper is improved." We are, he concluded, a "highly sentimental people."[7] A comment by Aviam Soifer can be used as a response to Stigler: "If there is often a humane tendency to lean in sympathy toward the poor, there may be a still stronger impulse for the rich to coerce the poor or for others to think it natural somehow for the rich to prevail."[8] This sense of the naturalness and appropriateness of things may extend to our own situations. Ian McEwan's novel *Saturday* includes this observation: "how restful it must once have been, in another age, to be prosperous and believe that an all knowing supernatural force had allotted people to their stations in life." And one would "not see how the belief served your own prosperity—a form of anosognosia, a useful psychiatric term for a lack of awareness of own's condition."[9] But that other age may also be our age. The meritocracy has created, sometimes as an alternative to a divine plan, the idea of the triumph of individual talent, skill and merit. If we are prosperous, we deserve that prosperity. And, if we are not, it is our failure.

At a time of extreme pessimism about the commitment of American society as a whole to a goal along the lines of universal security, there is a tendency to link this issue with others that are seen to divide the society. We sometimes suggest that it is all but impossible to generalize about what people across the board think. As to this, some comments of Alexander Pekelis are a useful corrective. Viewing the America of his time, the late l930s and early l940s from the perspective of a recent immigrant with early experience in Tzarist Russia and a later career in Italy, Pekelis saw that there was a notable consensus in the United States on some points. He wrote:

---

human mind, as it is written: For the earth shall be full of the knowledge of the Lord, as the waters cover the sea (Isa. 11:9). Quoted in Ayreh Botwinick (2001), "Maimonides Messianic Age", *Judaism* Vol. 33, No. 4, (1984) 418–25, p. 420.

6 Marilyn Robinson (1980), *Housekeeping* (New York: Picador), p. 10.

7 George Stigler (1972), "The Law and Economics of Public Policy: A Plea to the Scholars", *The Journal of Legal Studies* 1: 1, 1–12.

8 Aviam Soifer (1995), *Law and The Company We Keep* (Cambridge: Harvard Univeristy Press), p. 171.

9 Ian McEwan (2005), *Saturday* (United States: Doubleday) pp. 73–74.

> It is only realistic to admit that our society has reached at least an outward agreement on an unprecedented number of issues. To begin with, infant mortality, continuous malnutrition of a large percentage of the domestic population, shelter and housing conditions promotive of disease and juvenile delinquency and even unnecessarily hazardous or degrading condition have no open advocates today.[10]

He reminds us pointedly that only recently, historically speaking, people argued publicly for slavery. But, perhaps more problematically, he also thought that "it is relatively safe to assume that very few people would publicly maintain today that society has no right or duty to provide for such adjustment of the income pattern as may be necessary to eliminate the worst forms of inequality."

It is as to this last that there may be doubt today, and yet it seems that there is something still in Pekelis's observation. Even those who would do little or nothing, for example, to directly deal with income redistribution, do not argue in the manner of Herbert Spencer that it is best that the poor simply die. Rather, they argue that their methods—whatever they are—will ultimately benefit everyone, including the poor and that other methods, what ever they are, will end up hurting the poor.[11]

Montaigne reports that cannibals visited the court of Charles IX and asked three questions, of which he could only remember two. The first concerned grown men being governed by a child. The second was prefaced by the idea that the cannibals had, in their language, a strange way of speaking of men as "halves of one another." The second question was, then "they had noticed that there were among us men full and gorged with all sorts of good things, and that their other halves were beggars at their doors, emaciated with hunger and poverty; and they thought it strange that these needy halves could endure such an injustice, and did not take the others by the throat, or set fire to their houses …"[12] Perhaps the third question was something along these lines: "What are you doing to fix all this?"

Thinking about change, one recalls the frustrations of H.G. Wells. "Measure with your eyes" he said to the Fabians, "this little meeting, this little hall … [t]hen, go out into the Strand. Note the size of the buildings and business places, note the glare of the advertisements, note the abundance of traffic and the multitude of people. Take a casual estimate of the site values as you go along. That is the world you are attempting to change."[13] It is no wonder that so many writers have gone in the

10 Alexander Pekelis (1970), *Law and Social Action* (ed. Milton Konvitz). (Ithaca, NY: Cornell University Press).

11 Still, however much they share his opposition to the New Deal there seem to be some today who would not find it possible to agree with Herbert Hoover's reference to the "'over swollen' fortunes [which] must be distributed through the pressure of taxes." Herbert Hoover (October 31, 1936), "The Challenge to Liberty, speech reported in the *New York Times* p. 4).

12 Michel de Montaigne (1989[1968]), "On Cannibals", in *Complete Essays of Montaigne* (trans. Donald Frame) (Stanford, CA: Stanford University Press), pp. 150–159.

13 H.G. Wells, "The Faults of the Fabians", quoted in Margaret Cole (1961), *Story of Fabian Socialism* (Stanford, CA: Stanford University Press), p. 120.

direction of the *deus ex machina* or the comet—inexplicable devices for transition—so that they will end up at "The Great Good Place".[14]

The impatience of Wells is supplemented by the idea that the social struggle must continue, the insistence, for example, of William Beveridge, who we are told, liked a line from Sophocles' *Antigone*: Accused by her sister of attempting the impossible, Antigone says that she will give it up "When my strength is gone, and not before."[15]

Again, one sees I.M. Rubinow, now in his last days, receiving a copy of his own book from Franklin Delano Roosevelt, signed by the President and with a striking inscription: "For the author—Dr. I. M. Rubinow. This reversal of the usual process is because of the interest I have had in reading your book."[16] But of course Roosevelt addressed a critic. Rubinow's response to the American social security program of the 1930s was grudgingly positive. It was "not altogether a failure" was the strongest endorsement he could manage; "… if one has taken literally the promises of a complete system of economic security, then the comparison of promise with performance must lead to deep disappointment." But at the same time, he thought that it was not necessary to see the future of such programs only in terms of the federal level. "What is important," he wrote, is that "the idea of a moderate prosperity plus security for all of us promises to replace the cannibalistic system of a constant competitive struggle."[17] And in this "struggle for a more peaceful social structure, must one put all one's hope in the source of federal authority?"[18]

As individuals ground security and their own futures in a realistic assessment of the institutions that are supposed to provide it, they may acquire a skeptical stance towards the claims of advocates and advertisers of all claims and ideologies. To the extent that this is a self-help book—more than a book of policy suggestions for government, though it has a suggestion—it is designed to assist the development of this stance. Sometimes people say about one idea or another, "I completely bought

---

14 A story by Henry James that imagines that place as a guest house without hosts, a cloister or monastery.

15 Jose Harris (1977), *William Beveridge* (Oxford: Oxford University Press).

16 Quoted on the Social Security Online website: www.ssa.gov/history/rubinow.html.

17 I.M. Rubinow (1936), "The Social Security Act: An Appraisal", *National Municipal Review* March, pp. 138–144. The reformers also disagreed with each other (on tensions with Abraham Epstein, see Roy Lubove, *The Struggle for Social Security*, p. 176).

18 Rubinow, id. See in general Ellen A. Peters (1998) *Capacity and Respect: A Perspective on the Historic Role of the State courts in the Federal System.* 73 (New York: University Law Review) 1065–1085. Noting that there are points in state constitutions which lack federal counterparts and illustrating with (among others) New York's constitutional provision for public support of the needy (New York Const. Art XVII sec 1) and New Mexico's provision of a fundamental right of "seeking and obtaining safety and happiness": N. M. Const. Art II sec. 4. The limit on state authority here is the federal supremacy clause. "Presumably, although a state constitutional provision may provide greater protection for individual liberties than an analogous federal provision, it cannot, under the Supremacy Clause, US Const., art VI, conflict directly with a federal constitutional mandate" (at 1068).

into it …" This is the sentence of women who trusted the altogether role-differentiated marriage of the 1950s—and then became divorcees with few marketable skills and no assets; of working men who trusted the company to honor their pension promises, promises carefully accompanied by some language to the effect that the pensions were at the will of the company; of beneficiaries of government benefits who thought that these would never be re-evaluated. The skeptical stance does not require heroism. It does, however, require some capacity to stand back from the cultures in which, finally, we are also always embedded, and a limited intellectual disengagement that is the precondition of the capacity to ask critical questions.

Index